Endorsements

Wendy Toliver... *Eden, Utah. Bestselling, award-winning novelist, and writing coach*

Each story is a true account a stranger making a positive difference in someone's life, how their kindness stayed a long while—perhaps forever—or, a time the author helped someone they didn't know. Have tissues near because these stories are sure to touch your heart and rekindle your faith in humanity.

Barbara Passaris Emanuelson... *Auburn, Maine. Author of historical and YA fiction, and personal narrative*

The stories kindle a yearning deep within, something catching fire and connecting us as human beings. In a time when life is difficult for many and there's so much suffering in the world, it's nice to know there's still good on Earth. I feel honored to be part of such a book and hope readers will enjoy this wonderful, timely collection.

Doug Gibson... *Retired journalist who lives in Ogden, Utah*

Everyone has a moment where an encounter with a stranger, someone you may not see again, changes your life for the better. *Fleeting Encounters*, shares experiences and inspiring stories you won't forget and will prompt you to recognize "fleeting encounters" in your own life.

Judy DeLong… *Ogden Valley, Utah*

A book of my heart! When reading, I had a smile on my face and a lump in my throat? These stories are incredibly heart-warming, so necessary, and waiting for you to discover. Hopefully, you'll remember times in your own adventures that changed lives.

Gerhard Hattingh… *Johannesburg, South Africa*

This anthology shows how life is all about love and influencing relationships and people's lives positively. These encouraging stories are a real inspiration showing caring for others. A great book for the times we live in.

Juli Robertson… *Pretoria, South Africa*

It's amazing how in an over-populated world, we still find strangers who touch our lives in a profound way. We hold onto those memories for years to come. Sometimes, these fleeting encounters make us realize there are angels helping ease our pain and assisting us through difficult times. Many stories within will tug at the heartstrings in this feel-good, touching collection of personal experiences.

Janet Batisti… *Avid Reader. Ogden, Utah.*

We all have brief encounters. Some stand out and make an impression on us… this book is full of those. The stories will leave you in awe. The talented authors behind these stories are amazing.

Fleeting Encounters

Drienie Hattingh

Acknowledgements

My utmost thanks go to the authors who contributed their wonderful true, inspiring stories to this anthology. How amazing it was to open emails and read touching, sometimes heart-wrenching stories, (making me cry and smile), from nineteen authors. They answered my call for true stories about fleeting encounters with strangers that somehow changed their lives.

Thank you, Alex, Anne, Barbara, Carolyn, Celeste, Christy, Dimitria, Doug, Eugene, Karen, Lynda, Margaret, Marley, Mary, Mette, Penny, Sherry, Terry, and Wendy. Your stories inspired me to look at those around me, strangers, or not, with understanding and if needed, to show compassion. I am sure the readers of this little compilation will also be inspired to do the same.

Kudos to my dear friend, Barbara Emanuelson, *Educator, Author of adult historical fiction, YA historical fiction/fantasy.* She has been a constant inspiration and continued help with my books through the years. When it came to crunch time with *this* anthology, she was there too, brainstorming with me. I could send her a message and say, "Help," and she was there boots and all, helping with whatever was needed… be it, a final read through, or recommendations, or even, a last-minute story! I could not have done it without you, Barb. Forever Friends!

Thanks also to my trusted and extremely talented editor, Marley Gibson, who has been the editor of all seven of my books. This last couple of years has been extremely difficult for her with deaths in her family and severe health issues. Regardless, she kept on editing books. After she and her husband tested positive for COVID-19, I thought I would have to look for another editor. I was hyperventilating thinking no one would be able to fill Marley's shoes. She wrote to me and said, "Why would I not edit your book, I can still read!" That attitude personifies this amazing woman. Her total, ruthless honesty in editing my books makes it shine. That is not all… How amazing I can send off my manuscript to this miracle-worker… and a month later hold the finished book in my hands? Thank you for everything you do, Marley. You are my fairy-godmother-writing-angel.

My thanks to graphic designer, Dimitria Van Leeuwen, *Author, Graphic artist, and Musician,* who started working on this book's cover while in Mexico. Her talented art and enquiring mind have been responsible for the beautiful covers of all of my books, and those of my author friends. You are a true artist, Dimitria.

And, my never-ending gratitude to my forever friend, Wendy Toliver, *Bestselling, Award-winning novelist,* who has been there for me ever since I started writing fifteen years ago. She has read all of my manuscripts and gave me the confidence to keep on writing and get published. *Fleeting Encounters* was Wendy's idea... Calling me the anthology queen, she said *this* needed to be my next book. She also did the back copy of this anthology and wrote the introduction. Thank you, Wendy, you always have my back in *everything.*

Thank you to Janet Batisti, Judy DeLong, Barbara Emanuelson, Doug Gibson, Johan Hattingh, and Juli Robertson, for taking the time out of your busy schedules to read the manuscript. I appreciate you all, so much.

As always, my beloved Johan, have been by my side, encouraging me to keep on writing and praising my continued efforts. When I told him, in the midst of COVID times, that I wanted to do another anthology, he did not hesitate and said it was an amazing idea. I jokingly call him my manager… actually he is. I often ask his advice on my books, and he will brainstorm with me until my problem is resolved. I love this man no end… November will be our *50th* anniversary!

Last, but not least, I want to thank you, the reader, for choosing this anthology. I hope you enjoy the stories as much as I did and hope they will encourage you to spread kindness wherever life might take you.

Drienie

Table of Contents

Foreword

by Drienie Hattingh

Right from the start, I wanted this anthology to be published in November… *Thanksgiving month*. It would be difficult, I knew. It was the midst of COVID-19 and I could publish it later, but it was the perfect book for these times, bringing hope and encouragement.

However, would those I implored to write stories be inspired — or even be able — to contribute in these times? Would my editor be able to fit me into her schedule? What about my graphic artist?

I started feeling hopeful when stories began arriving daily. Authors wrote their fleeting encounters and their hearts overflowed with thankfulness, remembering those unforgettable chance meetings.

I knew those who would eventually read the stories would, in turn, feel the same and might even think back to similar incidents that filled their own hearts with gratitude.

The book was brimming with *thankfulness;* it had to be published *before* Thanksgiving. I heard back from my graphic artist, "Oooh... Can I put some ideas together?" and my editor, "I *will* make it work."

My initial idea was to fill it with true stories of people who had fleeting encounters with strangers that somehow changed their lives. Oddly, my premise for the book changed after I read the collective stories.

Suddenly, it dawned on me, *the stories were less about changing lives and more about the kindness of strangers.* I was awe-stricken as I pondered how certain patterns emerged and seemed to knit the stories together, even when told from such unique and different author perspectives. There was a universality in the stories and a clear theme threading its way through them all... **kindness**.

I'm not sure if I meant this to be the main theme in the stories, but I found this overwhelming sense of goodwill in almost every narrative, showcasing the essential kindness and willingness of people to help strangers. Doing good with nothing to gain. The selflessness of giving without question and how small acts, such as these, shaped lives for the better, for both the recipient and the giver. Stories which took place all over America… Arizona, California, Minnesota, New Jersey, North Dakota, North Carolina, Oregon, Utah… and even in other countries… France, Germany, Mexico, Nigeria, Peru, South Africa, and Kenya.

This does, indeed, prove that kindness is widespread and universal.

Introduction

by Wendy Toliver

Once I was in the checkout line at a grocery store when one of my sons threw a tantrum because I'd told him he couldn't have a candy bar. It wasn't a load of fun and I felt embarrassed because he was being so disruptive.

The lady behind me said, loudly enough to be heard over my son's yells, "I just want to applaud this mother. So many of us would've given in, just to make peace, but she's holding her ground. This world would be a better place if only more parents told their children 'no.'"

What happened next? People clapped!

The checkout guy, the people in line behind us, and the people standing in other lines—all of them were applauding. This confused my son, who had abruptly stopped having his conniption.

Now, this story isn't to illustrate how awesome I am at parenting—far from it—but to show when you're at your wits' end, sometimes all it takes is a supportive word from a stranger to turn everything around.

There's something special—magical, even—when a stranger shows us kindness. Perhaps it's because it's so unexpected. Or, because there are no strings attached. Maybe their altruism sparks giving in our heart and inspires us to do something nice for another stranger.

What's truly magical is you can show a stranger kindness in countless ways and never know how much of an impact an act of kindness can have on their life. Smiling at someone who seems downtrodden might brighten her day. Helping a couple change a flat tire can get them to their grandchild's basketball game on time. Leaving a server an extra-generous tip helps him pay his tuition. In some cases, a stranger's kind word or deed can even save someone's life.

Each story is a true account of how a stranger made a difference in someone's life and how their kindness has stayed with the recipient for a long while—perhaps, forever.

Have tissues nearby, because these stories are sure to touch your heart and rekindle your faith in humanity.

The pure relationship, how beautiful it is! How easily it is damaged, weighed down with irrelevancies--not even irrelevancies, just life itself, the accumulations of life and of time. For the first part of every relationship is pure, whether it be with friend or lover, husband, or child. It is pure, simple, and unencumbered. It is like the artist's vision before he has to discipline it into form, or like the flower of love before it has ripened to the firm but heavy fruit of responsibility. Every relationship seems simple at its start....

Anthologies published by Drienie Hattingh:

The Best Worst Christmas Ever

Tales from Ogden Canyon and Beyond

Tales from Two-Bit Street and Beyond, Part I

Tales from Two-Bit Street and Beyond, Part II

Tales from The Wasatch and Beyond

Strangers in the Night

by Drienie Hattingh

It was a sunny, cold December morning, twenty years ago, when we got into my SUV in Woodbury, Minnesota.

My mother, Ralie, and sisters, Elsabe and Sonja, were visiting us for two weeks in Minnesota from South Africa. They actually surprised me on my fiftieth birthday. I was in heaven, showing my beloved sisters and mother all my favorite places. Definitely on the list was my most favorite place in Minnesota: The North Shore of Lake Superior.

One of the goals on this specific road trip was to find snow. My sisters had never experienced snow and dearly wanted to walk in it, make snow angels, and build a snowman. It was early in December and had not yet snowed in the Twin Cities. So, when the weather people predicted snow on the North Shore, I told my sisters we were going and I booked us into one of our favorite hotels, the quaint Cove Point Inn, halfway up the scenic North Shore.

We did the one-hundred-and-fifty-mile trip on a beautiful cold blue-sky-Minnesota day and after about three hours, we stopped at the lovely harbor town of Duluth for lunch.

Still, no snow. However, we were hopeful as we continued up the shore, on Highway 61, the road to Canada. This highway is one of the most scenic in America. While living in The Twin Cities, Johan and I would often pile the children in the car and visit the North Shore in all seasons. We spent many a weekend on the shore visiting stunning places like Gooseberry Falls State Park, Kitchi Gammi Park, Temperance State Park, and Split Rock State Park. We would drive all the way to the Canada border and back, stopping for coffee, lunch, and dinner… admiring the beautiful scenery.

On this early winter's day, my sisters, our mother, and I marveled at the partly frozen waters of Lake Superior on our right and countless partly frozen waterfalls running into the lake.

As we snuggled under blankets in the car, my sisters *oohed* and *ahhed* at the quaint, beautiful, small towns, such as Two Harbors, Beaver Creek, Grand Marais, and Lutzen, all decorated for Christmas.

Our dear little mother had often travelled this road with me, during previous visits. Now she delighted in her two youngest daughters' obvious joy in observing the strange, to them, winter scenery and the scenic towns and majestic Lake Superior.

She kept saying, "I am sure we will soon see snow."

I fervently hoped she was right. If so, everything would be perfect. Snow would be the cherry on top.

We stopped several times at Lake Superior viewpoints. My sisters bought souvenirs and gifts for family back home. By dinner time, we arrived at Cove Point Inn. Still no snow.

After a wonderful walleye fish dinner, we took a walk on the beach admiring the early evening view over the seemingly endless Lake Superior. We pulled our warm coats closer to our bodies and tugged our hats further down over our cold ears and pushed our gloved hands deep into our pockets.

Sonja shivered and said, "I am sure it is going to snow soon. I just know it."

We smelled the smoke and heard *Silent Night* sung in German before we saw the delightful scene. A group of people sat around a blazing fire pit, dressed in brightly colored hats, scarves, and coats. I do not know if I had ever seen such a beautiful scene. The flames from the fire reflected warmly on their happy faces. I glanced at my sisters and our mother and I knew by the look on their faces they felt the same.

We stood silently enjoying the beautiful Christmas song, but then some of the singers waved at us and called out in strong German accents, "Come join us."

Someone pulled some logs closer to the fire and motioned for us to sit down.

We laughed and eagerly walked to the warming fire and sat down. They started to sing again and we listened in awe recognizing the Christmas songs, yet not understanding the words.

After a couple more songs, a woman asked where we were from and on hearing we were from South Africa, one of them asked, "Oh, are you Afrikaans?"

We nodded and then several people called out, "Sing some Christmas songs in Afrikaans."

We laughed, looked at each other, and started singing, "Silent Night" in Afrikaans... *"Stille nag, heilige nag..."* and followed with another favorite of ours, "Bethlehem Ster..." (Bethlehem Star.)

Tears welled up in my eyes at the wonder of this all. I could not believe I was there with my beloved sisters and my dear, dear Mother, sitting amongst complete strangers, in this beautiful place, singing our favorite Christmas songs.

Then, as if on cue, it started to snow.

Even now, twenty years later, the memory of that night—a fleeting encounter—is so clear I can feel the warmth of the fire on my face. Most of all, I remember the feeling of goodwill between complete strangers.

My beloved mother has been gone from us for several years now, so I thank God for wonderful memories such as the night when she sat around a crackling fire, on the North Shore of Lake Superior, with her three daughters, singing some of her favorite hymns in her native language.

The Wrong Address was the Right Address

by Wendy Toliver

I had an appointment with an orthopedic surgeon and mistakenly went to the wrong hospital.

Just after the hospital volunteer informed me I was in the wrong place, a woman in the lobby started chit-chatting with me. I kept thinking of ways to "escape" so I could still make my appointment. However, there was something in her eyes.

A sparkle, perhaps? A lilt in her voice?

Something in me shifted. I silenced all the noise in my head and opened my ears to her. I began *hearing* her.

"I had breast cancer. It didn't look good. To be honest, I was so tired. So over it all. Until today. My doctor just told me I am cancer free. Cancer free ..." She paused, almost as if tasting those last two words. As if they were chocolate-covered strawberries. Then, she laughed. She shook her head bashfully. "Goodness, I hope you don't mind me spilling my story all over you like this. You know, other than my doctor and nurse, you're the first person I've told. I hope you don't mind. I couldn't keep the news to myself."

I know I didn't deserve to be *that* person. But, for some reason, I was.

We hugged.

I don't know who initiated it. It didn't matter.

We jumped up and down, not caring who saw.

"You're cancer free!" I shouted, and I could feel my heart opening wide.

People looked at us. Some smiled. I kind of hoped someone would cheer, but no one did. It didn't matter. I celebrated with her. Then, we left the lobby side-by-side, walked into the cloudy winter day, and got in our respective cars.

I was late to my appointment across town. Very late. The receptionist didn't turn me away. The surgeon worked me in to his schedule. They treated me with the utmost kindness, no questions, no judgment.

I don't know why a stranger chose to tell *me* her miraculous news. Yet, I'm glad she did. I wonder if she realizes how touched I was and how it reminded me to step back and see The Big Picture.

It's a reminder we all need from time to time.

Gas Station Heroine

by Mette Harrison

It had been six months since I'd seen my ninety-year-old mother; not since my father's funeral at the start of the COVID-19 pandemic. Since I was quarantining, I wasn't driving my car or keeping up with maintenance—oil, gas—like I normally did.

Imagine my surprise when I was almost halfway to Provo and saw the "Low Gas" light flashing at me. I didn't know how long it had been on, but I figured I'd better take the next exit and get to the gas station as soon as possible.

When I pulled up to the pump, I realized I didn't have my wallet. I'd forgotten that normal part of life, too.

I hadn't been using money. Everything I bought tended to be online deliveries or grocery pickup. So, trying not to curse, I thought about what to do.

After a moment, I walked into the gas station and told the clerk I'd come out without my wallet and I wondered if I could punch my credit card number into the machine since I had it memorized.

"No, it doesn't work that way," she said.

"Oh," I said, trying to think of another solution. I wondered if I could offer to send her money through an online app. I had my phone, so I could certainly do that.

"I could lend you my card," she said. "You could come pay me back when you travel this way again."

I processed her offer. *Who lends out their credit card to a stranger?*

"Um, that would be very kind. Thank you," I said in shock.

Because… what else could I say? If I didn't take up her offer, I was in for a long walk or asking relatives to go really far out of their way to come rescue me.

The clerk got out her wallet and looked through a number of cards before handing me one. "Go on. Take that one."

I explained to her I was going to visit my mother and asked if I could send her a check when I got home because, otherwise, it would be a long drive back.

She considered it, then nodded. She wrote out her name, Lejeanne, address, and phone number. "Just in case," she said, and handed it to me. "Go on," she said.

I went out and tried to fill my car, but something was wrong with the pump, so I moved it to another pump to see if it would work.

Lejeanne came out. "Oh, I thought you'd driven off," she said. "Here I was thinking you looked honest."

"The pump wasn't working," I said hurriedly. "Sorry to scare you."

She fixed the pump and I used her card. When finished, I walked back in to return it to her. "I'll send the money as soon as I get home, I promise."

I enjoyed an afternoon chatting with my mother and sisters. When I told them the story, my mother went inside her apartment and came out with a twenty-dollar bill. "Hide it in your car," she said.

"I'll be fine," I insisted.

My mother wasn't having any of it. "I'm not going to be able to sleep tonight if you don't go put that money in your car, so I won't worry about you," she insisted.

So, I got home with twenty extra dollars in cash and a car full of gas, thinking of how good people are in the world and how lucky I was.

I went to work figuring out what I could send the gas station angel that would be an appropriate thanks other than the money I owed her.

I mailed my repayment with enough for her to have a nice dinner, plus a note with my eternal gratitude.

A Flight to Remember

by Anne Sinno

My phone rang while I was having dinner with a co-worker during a business trip in Portland, Oregon in September 2013. It was my dad calling from Minnesota.

The news was devastating. My mom had a stroke. The local Fergus Falls, Minnesota hospital told the ambulance to take her directly to Fargo, North Dakota. She was out of brain surgery and should wake up in the morning.

"The doctor said the next twenty-four hours will be crucial," Dad informed me.

All alone in my room later that night, I heard the pouring rain outside my window. My thoughts went back to earlier in the year when my mom and I were at this same hotel and I saw her walking in the rain wearing my raincoat. I smiled remembering how she adjusted the belt to fit her smaller frame. She had teased me about how I didn't tell her it would rain the whole trip.

I got up after spending a restless night, went through the motions of getting dressed, and went to the airport. I had not heard from my dad yet and I was afraid to call him.

At the airport, on my way to Salt Lake City for my next work event, I felt numb as I peered around at the gate area. It seemed everyone was busy doing nothing. Then, I noticed the gate right next to me was a flight to Fargo. My heart raced, my hands were sweating, a feeling came over me that something was terribly wrong, and I had to get to Fargo *now*. I immediately got on the phone, cancelled my meetings, and arranged to get on the flight to Fargo.

I called to tell Dad I would be there at five p.m., ready to insist if he said not to come. For the first time in my life, I heard despair in his voice, then he told me the horrific news. Mom didn't wake up as expected. She was still in a coma. Suddenly, I felt terribly angry. Why did this have to happen to my wonderful, healthy mom?

I walked into the airport bathroom.

My reflection seethed back at me.

I had to do something.

I kicked the trash can, not realizing it was metal and attached to the wall.

My foot hurt like hell and now I was even angrier... my tears were not because of my hurting foot.

When Dad picked me up at airport in Fargo later that day, we stayed strong for each other. Be positive. Even though I was the farthest away geographically, I was the first of my four siblings to arrive.

I felt a shock going through my whole body on entering the huge hospital room. My heart broke when I saw my mother lying on her back, in the one corner of the room, surrounded on all sides with countless machines, connected to her. She looked so small, but she looked as if she was sleeping, as if nothing was wrong with her. Constant beeping noises filled the room, and there was nothing personal anywhere. Not even one flower or plant. The one whole wall was covered in windows, but this did nothing to brighten the room. The whole scene was very cold.

After praying together, our family stayed strong the next couple of days, and then we had to make a heart-wrenching decision.

"We're taking her off life support...as per her wishes." Her body was so strong, but the stroke killed her brain.

The doctor thought she would last only one or two hours once the life support was removed but the agony went on for eight days. After we each had our time alone with her, all twelve of us sat on hard chairs around her hospital bed taking turns to leave for a quick nap on a bigger chair in the waiting room.

In the midst of our sorrow close family friends, who owned the ambulance company in our small town, offered to transport our beloved mom to a local nursing home, into a warm, cozy room on the first floor near the entrance door. It softened our heartache to have her in the town where she and our dad lived, in kinder surroundings where we could hang out with her until she let out her final breath.

Every now and again, I'd think, *how is this all possible? Everything is carrying on as usual. How can the world just keep on turning?*

The next few weeks were grueling. I was the last one to leave Dad as I finally went home to Arizona. It broke my heart leaving him alone in the big house my mom had always taken such good care of while he was always working. Mom used to do everything in the house, cleaning, washing, cooking. Dad took care of everything else, the yard, the cars, fix what was broken. Now, he was on his own and would have to do everything.

While staying with him, I tried to show him how to *keep* house. I physically demonstrated how Mom cleaned and showed him how to prepare simple meals. I even had to show him how to make coffee from the filter, to the grounds, to the water.

He is a retired highway patrolman, I thought. *He knew how to do and fix everything. How is it possible he can't make coffee or turn on the washing machine?*

As I hugged him, I knew deep down that even after showing him how to do all of those things, he would probably not. As I rode away, one of the main thoughts circling around my mind was, *how will he cope?*

When I took my seat on the plane later, I opened a bag filled with items I had taken from my old bedroom… books and papers with special meaning to me. Suddenly, I came upon a book so incredibly special to my mom and me, *Miss Rumphius.* Mom used to read it to me, and I have read it several times on my own ever since. This book was filled with beautiful artwork of a lovely Maine village and the most amazing purple lupine flowers. I loved the true story of how a young girl wondered all of her life—after her grandfather told her she would do something special one day—*what* that special something would be, only to discover in her old age how she was meant to beautify her small village by spreading lupine seeds everywhere. This would make the whole area bloom with purple flowers every year.

My hand stroked the worn front cover softly. Tears welled up in my eyes blinding my vision. I'd kept the tears from spilling for the last two weeks, but now they came in floods. After using all my tissues, I embarrassingly started sobbing uncontrollably. Between sobs, I noticed fresh tissues gently falling into my lap.

I turned to look at the woman next to me and all I could get out was, "My... Mother... j-j-just... passed."

I didn't need to say anything more. The look in her eyes said she understood; she must have been through something similar.

She put a hand over my trembling hands and, during the next couple hours, on our way from Minnesota, to Arizona, her words gave me hope and comfort at a time when nothing made sense.

***

I often reflect on the fleeting encounter with my Airplane Angel. I know my mom sent her to comfort and console me. Seven years later, I still miss Mom, but I am comforted by so many happy memories and I thank God for those.

I often think of our last conversation. I talked to her right before her stroke occurred, which made me the last person to talk to her. We didn't say anything profound; it was an ordinary discussion about everyday stuff. Yet, I feel comfort in the fact we ended the conversation, as always, with, "I love you."

l still wear the raincoat she had on that rainy day in Oregon, adjusted belt and all.

The Bach Badinerie

by Christy Monson

I rifle through my drawer, looking for my white Sunday socks. The new pair I got for my eighth birthday.

"Hurry." Mother pokes her head in my bedroom door. "We need to leave in a minute."

"Coming," I find my socks and slip them on followed by my black-patent leather Mary Jane shoes.

I smooth my new white dress with yellow butterflies embroidered around the hem. I twirl and the skirt flies out. I feel like a princess. I pull on my white gloves and skip out the door.

Mother and I climb into our black 1949 Chevy. It's three years old, but it seems like a new car because Mother takes such good care of it.

Mother and I are going to a concert like two grown-ups. She parks in the lot beside Ogden High School, a fancy yellow-brick building with four floors of tall windows lined up in a row like soldiers. Three arches divide the grand entry way into sections. Mother always said it was the first million-dollar high school in the country, but I don't know if that's true.

We pull the doors open and climb the marble stairs to the balcony. People are talking and laughing—like a party. I smile up at Mother. The usher glanced at our tickets, hands us a program, and guides us to our seats. I breathe in the excitement of being in the large auditorium, sitting in the first row of the balcony. I can lean on the railing and see everything.

The orchestra is warming up. Every single player is practicing something different. It sounds like a big mess. I'm glad when they quiet down.

The person playing the oboe stands and sounds a tone. The first violins match it, then the second violins and the rest of the strings, followed by the woodwinds and brass. A shiver of anticipation slides through me.

The conductor comes to the podium. Everyone claps. Then, he holds his hand out to bring someone else on stage. A flute player. The flutist is not too tall and has sandy hair. His instrument is gold. I stare at it. I've only seen silver ones. What will a gold flute sound like?

I gazed at the program. He will be playing *Badinerie* by Johan Sebastian Bach. The conductor raises his arms. The orchestra members sit tall and begin to play. The flute and orchestra blend. The music is fast, like a twirling dance.

The sound is golden like his flute. It fills the auditorium and swirls around me into my body and lands in my heart. I had never heard anything so lovely.

"Oh," I breathe out. "It's wonderful."

Mother smiled at me.

I listen to the notes going up and coming down and the trills. I'm so happy, I could float away up into the starry night and never come down.

When I get home, I tell mother I want to play the flute. "It's the most beautiful instrument in the world."

"Next year you can begin band," Mother says. "The flute is a great instrument."

The *Badinerie* stays in my head and I replay the memory often. I didn't ever meet the not-too-tall, sandy-haired flutist, but his music is in my heart. (It's safe to say, since I still remember it fifty years later and will probably always be with me.)

The next year, I got a flute for my birthday. I started lessons, but I didn't sound like the flutist. I was having fun playing it and I practice every day. In my grade are two other girls, Debbie and Charlotte. They play the flute, also. We become fast friends. We practice together and play duets, with two of us taking one part, and sometimes trios (when we can find them).

We attend junior high together where I learned to play the piccolo for the marching band. We hated the uniforms because they were made of heavy wool.

Two of us end up in college together, still marching in the band for football games. We played in the concert band and the orchestra

During my senior year at the university, the orchestra director asks if I would like to play a solo with the group. I tell him I would love to and choose the Mozart *Flute Concerto #2 in D Major*. What an honor. I loved that experience.

I go on to win the Utah State Fair Music competition and I solo with the Utah Symphony in both Logan and Ogden, Utah. My teacher helps me choose the music… The *Badinerie* by Bach, of course.

Oh, what joy comes from playing the piece that stole my heart so many years ago when I was a child.

Nothing can compare with the feeling of accomplishing a dream.

Music gave me many wonderful opportunities, but the best will always be playing the Bach *Badinerie* with the Utah Symphony.

What an influence the flute soloist had on my life.

I believe we encounter many people who have an impact on us, and we, in turn, influence other people's lives for good. As we develop our talents and share them with the world, we can make a difference in the lives of those around us.

I gained lots of good friends—Debbie and Charlotte are still my buddies—and have had wonderful experiences—all because of the *Badinerie*.

The Bus Driver Angel

by Celeste Kuun

Have you ever been to Bergen County in New Jersey? Did you even know there was a Bergen County in New Jersey? It is not a particularly special county or extraordinarily picturesque. I will excuse you for not carrying any knowledge of Bergen County in New Jersey because until June 2005, I lived my life in blissful ignorance of Bergen County, New Jersey and the Ramada Inn within its confines.

Let me explain.

In 2005, I'd graduated high school in Johannesburg, South Africa. Rather than committing to a university course to determine my career for the next thirty-odd years of my life, I decided to go on a Big Adventure.

I wanted to see the world.

My foray into the unknown started in the good ol' United States of America as a summer camp counselor. To most Americans, summer camp is a part of life. Millions of American children look forward to making summer memories at camp every year (and for good reason), without sparing a single thought to the unique camping experience. However, summer camps are so quintessentially American that it was virtually unknown in countries outside of the U.S. in 2005.

Thankfully, my family was in a financial position to send me to America to experience life from a different perspective.

I applied through an agency based in Fourways, South Africa (don't worry, I definitely don't expect you to know South African geography). The agency sent my application off to a number of camp directors and telephonic interviews happened. Then weeks of agonized waiting followed.

My phone rang on May 20th:

"Hello, Celeste. This is Darren from Camp Agency," the voice on the other end of the line said. I was so nervous; I only uttered an "uh huh" as acknowledgement.

"It is my pleasure to inform you that your application was successful," said Darren. "Camp Canonicus in Rhode Island would love to welcome you as an international staff member in the summer."

I was stunned into silence… something that happens infrequently. Poor Darren had more of a monologue than a dialogue.

And with that, my Big Adventure had started.

A subsequent e-mail contained instructions on what to do once touch down happened: *I was to get on a bus at JFK International Airport and head toward the Port Authority terminal in Manhattan. From there, I was to purchase a ticket to East Bergen in New Jersey. Once there, I was to get off at the Ramada Inn.*

All of this sounded so thrilling and exotic. I completely forgot to be nervous.

On June 3rd, I waved goodbye to my family, stepped onto a plane, and spent the next sixteen hours headed toward North America. By the time we touched down in New York, I was glad to breathe outside air. I had a special mission to complete.

Finding the bus to Port Authority was the easy part. A security guard at the airport made finding the correct bus stop a breeze.

Navigating the bus terminal, however, was an entirely different kettle of fish. The bus terminal was massive with thousands of commuters who all seemingly knew where to go. I found a ticket counter, as good a place as any to start, in my opinion.

"Hello, I would like to purchase a ticket to East Bergen, New Jersey, please," I said to the ticket agent. She tapped away at her keyboard.

"There is no East Bergen in my system," she said.

"That can't be. I need to be at the Ramada Inn in East Bergen," I said, holding up the e-mail as proof that yes, East Bergen truly did exist. She stared at me blankly.

"Next," she shouted. With that, I was dismissed.

I looked at my watch. I had to be at the Ramada Inn to meet my camp director in one hour. I had no idea how far New Jersey was from where I was currently.

I made my way to a wall of pay phones (yes, they were still a thing in 2005) and dialed the camp's number.

I explained to the extremely sweet receptionist how I was stuck in New York with no idea how to get to this hotel that didn't exist, according to the ticket agent. I was awfully close to tears.

"Well, dear, you still have some time to get there. The directors got a bit lost on the way to New Jersey.

They will only be at the hotel in two hours," the receptionist explained.

That bought me a precious couple of hours to get to the Ramada Inn.

The receptionist took my number and ordered me to wait by the payphone while she made a few calls.

I waited. As I stood there, surrounded by strangers, and so far from home, I knew I was very much out of my comfort zone. It was nerve wracking but exhilarating at the same time.

Even though I was worried, I marveled at the new sights around me… and the accents.

This, I reminded myself, *is all part of the adventure.*

The phone rang after ten minutes.

"What did you say the address is, dear?" she asked.

"I don't know the address, but it's the Ramada Inn in East Bergen," I said.

A bus driver who had alighted from his bus to go to the restroom passed at that very moment, overhearing my conversation.

He tapped me on my shoulder. "My route goes right by the Ramada Inn. I can take you," he said.

I relayed the message to the receptionist on the phone, thanked her for her help, and followed the bus driver to his bus. He did not charge me for the trip to the Ramada Inn.

The bus driver stopped right in front of the Ramada Inn just as Camp Canonicus' van bumped into the drive.

I had the best summer of my life that year.

Do you know what serendipity is? It is a bus driver needing a comfort break right when I was at the verge of an emotional breakdown.

For those of you Googling the Ramada Inn in East Bergen, do not bother. It does not exist.

The Ramada Inn in question is in Rochelle Park near Paramus.

Regardless, I will always be thankful for a bus driver who took the time to speak to a lost and confused South African.

Feeling Thankful and Guilty in Lutzen

by Drienie Hattingh

Many years ago, when we lived in Minnesota, my husband, Johan, and I spent a week on the North Shore of Lake Superior, staying at a self-contained unit at Lutzen, one of the idyllic little towns dotting the North Shore. After unpacking, I went to the grocery store for supplies.

When I approached the last aisle, I saw how my cart was completely loaded with essential household items, fruits, vegetables, bread, cereals, and salads. Hoping it would not fall off the cart, I grabbed our favorite two-layers-of-softness toilet paper and placed it on top of the pile. I saw an elderly lady puzzling over every type of toilet paper on the shelf as if it were a very difficult decision. She reminded me of my grandmother, Ouma Mouton, with her gray hair tied in a bun in the nape of her neck. She wore a lovely burgundy coat and sensible low-heeled shoes to match. Her outfit was completed by a matching little purse hanging in the crook of her one arm. Eventually, she took the cheapest four-pack... the one-layer type, which I found strange.

I hurried as I glanced at my watch. Johan and I planned to have a sunset barbecue on our deck which faced the majestic Lake Superior

I fell in line at the till. Many carts were loaded to the brim, like mine. Right in front me, though, was the One-Layer Lady. At first, I was happy to see her cart was only about a third full. She would move through quickly and I would be in time for my date with Johan.

All of a sudden, I felt weirdly selfish and sad as I watched her unpacking the cart. Some items she placed on the counter were similar to mine, but it was of lesser quality... cheap bread, one-layer toilet rolls, regular fruits and vegetables, and less volume than mine. Certainly, no unnecessary things, like candy, chips, or cookies.

I could not take my eyes off her gnarled hands unloading every item with the utmost care. My heart almost broke when she saw the final amount on the till. With huge, shocked eyes, she opened her tiny purse and started counting out money.

I could not take it any longer.

In one swift move — while the lady wasn't looking — I gave the cashier my credit card. The girl appeared shocked, at first, and then her eyes turned to understanding and she put her hand on the lady's arm and leaned forward to talk to her.

She glanced at me while she talked and saw me shaking my head from side-to-side and mouthing, "No!" She nodded in understanding. I did not want the woman to know I was paying for her groceries.

I had no idea what the cashier said to the lady, but her face lit up and she dazzled me with the most angelic smile as she put her money away.

While the cashier bagged the groceries, I slipped in the chocolate cake from my cart. The clerk understood, rang it up, and sneaked it into the lady's bags.

I looked around and was happy no one seemed to notice what had happened between me and the cashier.

When it was my turn to pay, the cashier thankfully did not discuss what happened. However, she took my hand and squeezed it.

When I walked out of the store, I passed the old lady closing her trunk. She glanced up at me and we shared a smile.

"God bless you," she said before she turned and climbed into her car.

"You too," I murmured.

When I returned to our vacation rental, Johan had the barbecue fired up.

"You're just in time for a magnificent sunset," Johan called out. "How did your shopping go? Did you get all we needed?"

Gosh, that sort of got to me. We *did not* need half of what I purchased.

"Yes," I said, "I got more than we need!"

After a wonderful dinner of bratwurst and potato salad, we watched darkness settle over Lake Superior. We listened to waves lapping on the shore and ate our vanilla bean ice cream.

"You should have gotten a cake," Johan said.

"I guess…" I said with a shrug.

I hope the lovely lady enjoyed the chocolate cake.

Where Are You Headed?

by Mary Pettersen

Voyageurs National Park in Northern Minnesota had many more visitors this past summer due to COVID-19. Instead of flying to their destinations, a lot of summer travelers enjoyed our National Parks for the first time.

My husband, Mark, and I have had our cabin on Crane Lake, the entrance to the Park, for twenty-seven years and have travelled to our favorite fishing spots hundreds of times. We know every submerged rock (and there are many), every hidden bay, and every fishing hole where the walleyes and crappies are waiting for us to dangle a minnow.

On this sunny morning, we headed from Crane Lake through King William's Narrows into Sandpoint Lake and down The Little Vermillion, a narrow stretch of water resembling a river connecting Sandpoint Lake to the Loon River and Lac La Croix beyond. The water was like a mirror in the early morning sunshine. On this chain of lakes in Voyageurs National Park, Canada is on one side and Minnesota on the other. The International Border doesn't necessarily go down the middle of the lake or river. You have to follow the map. Ordinarily, Americans wanting to fish in Canadian waters would stop in their boats at Canadian customs right on Sandpoint Lake.

However, this year, because of COVID-19, *no one* can enter Canada. Not even Americans who have cabins on the Canadian side. So, we were very careful to stay far into U.S. waters on these border lakes.

We took advantage of the still water and went as fast as we dared, gliding around the many curves. As our motorboat rounded one, we noticed three, shiny, red canoes paddling into a bay on the glassy water.

I was about to get my phone out to capture the picturesque scene when my husband suddenly slowed our boat and turned off the motor.

"Where are you headed?" he shouted out to the paddler closest to us.

"Crane Lake" was his reply. I noticed his fellow canoeist had a map in her lap.

"You've got to turn around," my husband informed them. "That bay takes you into Canada."

They had evidently mistaken the narrow Little Vermilion Lake for King William's Narrows.

Mark said, "You've got to go all the way back to Sandpoint Lake, then hug the south shore and you'll see King William's Narrows. That'll take you to Crane Lake."

The six canoeists looked at each other and probably decided by our outfitted fishing boat and our grey hair we had been around the lakes a couple of times and knew our way around. They thanked us many times over, turned their canoes around, and headed down the long stretch of water.

On our way back to our cabin with a mess of crappies, we sped past the national park campsite on Crane Lake hoping to see those three shiny red canoes. And, sure enough, there they were.

With our hair flying in our faces, Mark and I nodded at each other like two mother hens knowing their chicks were safe in the nest.

Butterscotch, Bandits, and all that Jazz

by Margaret Zeemer

It is said Africa speaks to the Soul. When you leave Africa, part of your soul is left behind, patiently waiting for your return.

My heart pounded as I stood on the fore deck of the luxurious ocean liner bringing me back here. I watched the approaching lights of shore as the African sun slowly rose in the East behind us with the promise of another glorious day.

Mombasa, Kenya lies on the East side of this great continent with 333 miles of coastline on the Indian Ocean. As the ship glided majestically into the Kilindini

Harbour, the largest Seaport on the East coast of Africa, I made my way back to my stateroom to collect my bag.

I waited impatiently for the ship to clear Customs. Finally, I made my way down the gangway and, once more, step onto the soil of Africa.

The Port of Kilindini was always crowded. Commercial seagoing vessels, loading and unloading their wares from faraway places, porters and supply trucks ready to offload supplies to the great cruise ships that dock daily, tourists of every nationality hurrying toward their buses, eager to get a glimpse of the Big Five—lions, leopards, rhinoceros, elephant, and Cape buffalo—hundreds of local people selling their souvenirs, artwork, and carvings spread across the pavement so that not a square inch of space remained.

It all would have to wait for me today as I picked my way through the throng to the gates of the Port and the ride that would take me to my adventure for the next three days. *Amboseli National Game Reserve.*

I'd booked a car and driver to take me to Amboseli. He was a handsome young man named Richard. Dressed in crisp, white shirt and neatly pressed khaki trousers, Richard showed me his identification, retrieved my bag, and said "Follow me, madam. We go to the car."

Our vehicle was a new-looking minibus with enough room for ten people. Richard loaded my bag, opened a sliding door on the side of the van, and in I climbed. I was the only passenger.

We're on our way. It won't be too long now.

As we left the bustling, dusty streets of Mombasa behind, I asked Richard, who spoke excellent English, "How long will the trip to Amboseli take us?"

"It will take about ten hours," he said, showing perfect white teeth in a smile as broad as his ebony face.

"Ten hours?" I must have looked horrified as he hurriedly explained how Amboseli was 280 miles to the east of Mombasa and part of the journey would take us through the bush country of the Maasai. Amboseli Reserve was managed and operated by the Maasai, the largest in Kenya and a prime reason I wanted to go there.

The Mombasa Highway was the main route between Nairobi, the capital city, Mombasa. It was jokingly called the *Mambo* Highway due to the large number of potholes and deep ruts causing the traffic to bounce and sway left and right. Toxic fumes belched from the hundreds of trucks and lorries making their way back and forth to the port.

Richard was a great driver and I soon relaxed enough to release my grip on the dashboard.

We finally left the Highway from hell after a few hours and turned onto another smaller road signposted to Tsavo East, another sprawling Game Reserve, known for its elephant orphanage center. Not much later, we pulled through the gates of the Reserve where Richard announced my lunch would be served.

I was shown into the magnificent central three-story lodge held up by massive posts of elaborately carved timbers. Open along the length of one side, the dining room overlooked the lush Game Reserve where elephants languished in large drinking holes, splashing their backs with their trunks. Water Buffalo and Zebra were also there, as well as an enormous variety of beautiful birds. I could not stop staring at this amazing scene.

I turned to ask Richard where he would like to sit, but he was not there.

I stopped a passing waiter to ask where he had gone and was met with an embarrassed and puzzled expression.

"He's not permitted in here, ma'am," and quickly turned away.

My lunch was not so enjoyable after that.

***

Following eating, I met Richard outside and asked him if he would allow me to ride up front with him. At first, he seemed uneasy, but we started chatting and he shared stories of his three children, who had never seen *any* of the wildlife of Africa, only in picture books.

We set off across country. As the trees began to thin out, so did the condition of the road. Recent rains had washed much of the pavement away and we were, once again, doing the Mambo crawl as we picked our way into the African bush… completely alone. The sun was high in the sky by now and no animals were to be seen.

Eventually, we pulled into a small grove of trees, where to my surprise, I saw a group of twelve men ahead of us. They were soldiers in faded brown, dusty uniforms, each with a weapon of some sort draped across a shoulder. They seemed to be guarding a rusty metal barrier closed across the road. They made no move to approach us or even acknowledge we were there.

Richard turned off the engine and sat there. I looked at the soldiers, then at Richard, and back at the soldiers again, wondering what on earth was happening. My heart was pounding so loud, surely these men could hear. I prayed silently they would not suddenly become interested in our lone vehicle parked under the trees. I dug my fingernails into the woven upholstery of the seat as I watched, slightly terrified and praying the soldiers would not approach us. Would they want a bribe from me to get through?

Do I have enough cash to buy my freedom?

My mouth was dry as I turned to my silent driver and gulped, "Okay, Richard... what exactly is going on here? Why aren't we driving?" I finally asked. It didn't help to see Richard chewing a fingernail as he watched the group of soldiers standing under the shade of a tree, smoking cigarettes and laughing.

"It is the law in Kenya we must wait for an armed police escort to cross into Maasai territory," he said, not making eye contact. "There are bandits," he added.

I gulped again. *Why was I not told this when I booked this trip?* The thought raced through my head as I frantically calculated my odds of survival. "Should we go back to Mombasa?" I asked.

"No, no, madam" he said, glancing sideways at me. "It will be safe with the guard."

Not the least bit convinced, I glanced around at the small clearing hoping this guard would arrive soon.

The minutes ticked by as my apprehension grew stronger.

Margaret! What are you doing out here? I asked myself. *There will be no adventure if you are not alive to tell anybody about it.*

After what seemed like ages, I noticed movement from behind a small wooden hut off to my left and wondered what new terror was coming now.

Another man appeared and glanced at our vehicle with a scowl. He pulled a dirty red rag from the back pocket of his wrinkled blue jeans and wiped it across the sagging, black skin of his face and neck.

Shouting words—which I did not understand—to the guards at the barrier, he picked up a bulky automatic rifle propped against the hut and slung it across his shoulder. As he started to move, a long, steel machete, hanging from his waist, banged against his leg.

He walked sluggishly toward us.

At first, he stood by the minivan and glared at me sitting in the front with Richard. A few angry words in a native tongue exchanged between them and the man finally opened the door and climbed in behind me.

Oh boy, nothing like having a bodyguard who hates you at first sight.

We slid up to the barrier and the soldiers asked for our papers. Richard produced them and the barrier was lifted. Once again, we set off into the wilderness, this time with a reluctant, angry passenger on board.

I was miserable as we bounced along again. Occasionally, the two men exchanged words in Swahili to the point I was convinced they were talking about this strange white woman with flaming red hair traveling alone in bandit country. The tension in the bus was so thick you could slice it and I could tell Richard was not as relaxed and cheerful as he had been earlier.

The road became more rutted and washed out. Richard said it was due to recent flash flooding in the area, so we were forced to make detours around small lakes appearing where the road used to be. Richard was an excellent driver as he navigated the ruts and fissures, but I could not enjoy the journey as my fear of the strange, hostile man in the seat behind me flooded my thoughts and blinded my eyes to the beauty around me.

I rode in silence, barely daring to breathe and certainly could not turn my head to look at the wonders of Africa around me. I could think only of the automatic weapon a few inches from the back of my head.

It was right about then I had an epiphany. It was time to have a talk to myself.

Margaret, it seems you have two choices here. You are in this amazing land and here you sit, scared to death of the man behind you when there is nothing you can do about it right now. So, sit here like a frightened rabbit, eyes closed, not breathing, and clutching the seat or relax, cheer up, enjoy the ride, look around you at this magnificent land and be grateful.

No sooner had the thought come than I decided what to do. I took a deep breath, grew a new spine, put a smile on my face, and turned in my seat to face the guard.

I offered my hand to him and said, "Hi, my name is Margaret, what's yours?"

Unfortunately, I decided to do this shortly after he had fallen asleep. He awoke with a start, lunging toward me in his seat brandishing the automatic rifle in my face.

My newfound courage faded along with the last drop of color in my cheeks. Covering my head with my arms, I ducked.

Turned out, he didn't speak any English and it took some rapid talking from Richard to calm him down.

Onward, we bounced as my newfound bravery slowly returned and I rummaged into my backpack for my secret weapon.

Turning carefully this time, I held a small bag of butterscotch candy toward him.

"Take one," I said and nodded to him.

He grunted. His bloodshot eyes narrowing to slits as his gaze shifted between me and the bag. I took one out and put it in my mouth to show him they weren't poisoned and then handed one to him. This time, he took it and popped it into his mouth.

As the butterscotch-y wonderfulness apparently hit his tongue, he bobbed his head and grinned. I turned to Richard and gave him a sweet, too. Then, he shared how his tribe and the guard's tribe have been sworn enemies for generations, fighting against each other, and only calling a truce when it came to fighting a common enemy, the British.

I breathed in sharply, nearly inhaling the candy in and thinking, *had I told Richard I am from England?* I couldn't remember, but now I was determined to keep that tidbit to myself and work on my Yankee twang.

A few miles up the road, I felt a *tap-tap-tap* on my shoulder. I was used to passing the butterscotch treats back at a steady pace by now and was surprised when his long, muscular arm came forward pointing into the distance.

My thoughts immediately went to those back home who warned me to be careful, "There are bandits who roam the bush country. Travelers are regularly being captured, robbed, or worse."

My eyes frantically scanned the bush to see what horror my bodyguard was pointing at.

This is it… I thought, *my end is nigh…*

But, ever the optimist, I thought, *perhaps my butterscotch would save me again.*

I realized my bodyguard's eyes were a lot better than mine when I saw what he was pointing at.

"Oh wow!"

My heart jumped into my throat... Two magnificent giraffes. A mother and her baby eating leaves from the high branches of a tree.

They lazily gazed our way as we inched by, Richard decelerating for me to take photos.

What a thrill!

It was the first time I saw giraffe in the wild.

"Asante sana…" I said in Swahili to the guard.

On hearing my Swahili, a sudden look of surprise gave way to a bellowing laugh as he slapped at his lap and let forth with a whole string of expressions that made Richard and him laugh heartily.

Hmmmm... I didn't think my Swahili was that funny.

The ice was broken and Benjamin delighted in pointing out the increasingly abundant wildlife, even making Richard stop to show me a dung beetle rolling a large ball of elephant poop with its tiny back legs along the road.

***

At last, after my eventful ride from Mombasa, and to my absolute delight, we pulled into a Maasai village.

The Maasai were a tall and slender race and, even today, most lived in the traditional ways of their ancestors, still wearing the red and purple robes distinguishing them from other tribes.

Our vehicle was rapidly surrounded by dozens of villagers grinning eagerly at me through the dusty windows of the van and waving beaded necklaces, bracelets, and small wooden carvings.

Without a word, both Richard and Benjamin got out of the bus and left me sitting there.

What now? Another uh-oh moment?

A voice from the back of the crowd shouted out, "Hello, Mummy. Where you come from?"

Knowing full well they had no idea where Utah was, I said it anyway.

As one, their faces beamed with delight as they all sang out "Utah Jazz!" and "Carl Malone." They started doing a crazy jumping up and down dance, leaping into the air to amazing heights as the men waved long sharp poles in the air.

Leaving the village, we drove through a valley. Benjamin tapped on my shoulder and signaled straight before us. And there, rising out of the clouds, was the peak of the great Mt. Kilimanjaro, the highest peak in Africa. Still snowcapped, it dominated the entire surrounding landscape as it soared toward heavens.

"Asanta sana," I said with a smile. Few emotions rival the enormous swelling of the heart when one first lays eyes on a feature of our planet such as a great mountain.

"One day," I promised myself as I stared at the overwhelming sight before me. "I shall visit you, climb to your snowy peak, and thank you for watching over this beautiful plain."

Reluctant to leave this wonderful view, I climbed back into the van as we now faced our next challenge. We had to do the harrowing crossing over the gigantic plain of an ancient lava field formed during the countless eruptions of the volcano. Black, razor sharp volcanic glass and sharp-edged crevasses tore at the flimsy tires of our minivan, threatening to shred them at any moment. As the heat of the day rose out of the jet-black rock, we slowly inched our way across the lava.

The African sun was starting to go down as we arrived at the gates of Amboseli Game Reserve. Exhausted, yet somehow exhilarated, from the long, eventful journey, I had run through the entire gamut of emotions, feeling everything from utter terror to complete and utter joy. I was certainly not the woman who left Mombasa ten hours ago.

I spent this journey with two totally different, but incredibly amazing, African men and had the opportunity to get to know them in a way that in "my world" would never have happened. I overcame my fears and prejudices and met two kind and trustworthy human beings, and we were bonded by the common joy of laughter and butterscotch. Two humans on this planet I would never see again, but who helped change my world view and share some of theirs with me.

As Richard lifted my bags from the bus, Benjamin took me by the arm and motioned to my camera.

"You want a photo with me?" *How wonderful.*

So, there I was, in the glow of the African sunset, my bodyguard's heavy old automatic rifle cradled in my arms, and his arm around my shoulder.

"*Asante sana,*" I whispered as Richard captured the moment.

Yes, for sure, a part of my soul is still in Africa.

The Mystery Man in The City by The Bay

by Carolyn Campbell

I was in a different world.

I was five years old. For the first time, my parents took me along on an out-of-state vacation. The world of travel was familiar to them, new to me. During their marriage, they faced infertility for ten years before I became theirs through adoption. Afterward, they cradled me in a constant, comfortable cocoon of safety. Taking this trip was my first heady glimpse at adventure.

Mom and Dad sat on either side of me as we rode inside a cable car in Chinatown in San Francisco, California. I remember the slick feeling of the shiny wooden bench seats and the roller coaster experience of riding up and down San Francisco's famous hills.

The conductor rang a bell. Chains rattled, and the bell clanged. Yet something made me look upward. Within this foreign universe, I saw a tall, imposing man standing across from me. A long, loose gray coat draped his slim frame. He wore a dove gray felt hat. I had the sense of a powerful presence.

My imagination theorized he might be a wizard, a pharaoh, an emperor, maybe a maharajah or grand vizier. I was both afraid and intrigued. I couldn't look away.

When our eyes met, he stared into mine. For a moment, neither of us dropped our gaze. I thought I shouldn't stare, but he shouldn't either. He was the adult, I reasoned. Maybe it was okay for adults to stare at kids.

Finally, I lowered my eyes. I saw the mysterious man held a rounded object; a medallion. I studied the round silver piece clasped in his thin fingers. It was a long time before I glanced up again. When I did, he still stared at me.

My exposure to adults other than my parents was rare and new; I was intrigued and curious, but utterly unsure how to behave or react.

He held the medallion out to me, but not close enough where I could read it.

"Take it," he said.

Usually, my parents told me to take nothing from a stranger. Yet, as I glanced to the right, my mother nodded to me, the same unspoken way she communicated when she wanted me to use my fork or tie my shoe.

Despite her encouragement, I felt both brave and foolhardy as I reached forward. The man handed the medallion to me.

On inspecting it, I saw a single penny mounted in a round silver frame. The notation read, *"Keep me and never go broke."* The year on the penny was the same year I was born. Already, I knew the circumstances that led to my adoption constituted a mysterious, murky past I'd best leave alone.

How did he get a medallion from the year I was born?

"Say 'thank you,'" said my mom.

But, I couldn't.

The stranger and I stared at each other one more time. Then, the cable car jerked halfway up a hill. The man's gaze rose and I focused again on the medallion.

I will never forget that man.

And, for years, I wondered if I would someday find myself down on my luck, down to my last penny. If it happened, I speculated whether someone would accept the medallion as a desperate form of currency. I wondered if the mysterious man knew something I didn't. Maybe he knew the two of us had something in common. Though we hailed from different spheres, perhaps we each had a mysterious past.

Grandmothers

by Drienie Hattingh

During one of my many family visits to South Africa, I tried untangling a ball of yarn on the plane. I always knit on these long journeys to my country of birth. A seventeen-hour continuous flight can be awfully long and boring if you cannot somehow keep yourself busy. My grandmother, Ouma Stolz, who taught me to knit, always said, "Our hands must always be busy."

I watched several movies during those long flights… and I knit.

On this specific flight, I had the misfortune of having a huge ball of yarn that was totally tangled. When I pulled the starting point of the yarn, in the middle, like one is supposed to do, it was stuck. I yanked at it again, and as expected, the innards of the ball of yarn came forth in a huge, tangled mess.

I tugged the yarn apart, trying to unravel it with no success when the passenger next to me said, in a British English with a strong African accent, "Do you mind if I untangle your skein of yarn?"

I laughed and faced her. She was a beautiful woman, in her late sixties, like me, dressed in typical African attire. Her head was wrapped in a colorful bandanna and she wore a brightly colored cotton dress, twisted around her body in Nigerian fashion. She smiled warmly at me.

I said, 'Really? Are you sure? It's not fun, you know?"

"Oh, yes," she said. "I love untangling yarn. I would always do it for my grandmother while she knitted," she said with a melodious lilt in her voice.

I gratefully handed the colorful mess to her and watched as she went to work on it. I was mesmerized by her strong, long fingers moving through the gnarled yarn… it was as if she was directing an orchestra.

"That is beautiful," she said as she glanced at the rainbow-colored knitting in my lap. "A blanket?"

"Yes," I said. "It's for my grandson. He wanted a rainbow blanket."

"Oh," she said, her eyebrows raising in delight. "How many grandchildren do *you* have?"

"Two boys," I said.

She said proudly, "I have four."

During the next couple of hours, while she straightened out and I knitted, we talked about our grandsons and all their shenanigans. We shamelessly bragged about their accomplishments, like grandmothers are apt to do. Every now and again, we reached for our cell phones to show off photos of our beloved grandsons. The photos could not have been more opposite.

I looked in amazement at four African boys of different heights, smiling broadly as their grandmother took pictures of them. In some photos they wore perfectly ironed school uniforms and they stood in front of typical African-style thatched roofed dwellings, surrounded by dry countryside, dotted by thorn trees. In return, I showed her my grandsons playing in our townhouse backyard with lush green lawns and an abundance of brightly colored potted flowers and lush green trees. In some photos, my grandsons were dressed in jeans and T-shirts with their backpacks on their backs in front of huge school buildings, typical American kids. We both *ooohed* and *aahhed* at each other's photos.

When she finished her giant task, she reached down and extracted another ball of yarn from my knitting bag. She tugged at the same point I had, and again, a huge, tangled mess came forth. We both laughed as she went back to work.

The air hostess interrupted us every now and again, amused at the two of us, offering something to drink, at which we both would call out, "Tea, please."

We never talked about our children, only our grandsons and our hopes and dreams for them, their respective strong points, and what we thought they might become. She said her youngest grandson would make a good doctor and her oldest would be a veterinarian, the other two would make great teachers.

I told her my youngest was smart and extremely interested in space and would probably work at NASA someday. My oldest is exceptionally artistic and would be an accomplished artist one day.

She took the initiative and took all the yarn I had in my knitting bag and untangled each one that needed it. We chatted and chatted, and she untangled, and I knitted, and we never exchanged names.

Ultimately, the captain announced we were about to land in Gauteng, at the international airport in South Africa. We both looked at each other.

She voiced my thoughts. "That sure went fast."

I quickly gathered my knitting and other items and put them away. So did my friend. We gazed out the window as the early-morning sun broke across the ocean, tinting it in a deep orange.

Wow… I thought, *we never slept, we talked right through the night.*

When we landed, my friend immediately got up. She had a connecting flight to make and had to rush.

She bowed her head while her fingers closed around mine. "Thank you for a very enjoyable flight. Perhaps we will meet again someday. God be with you and your grandsons."

I squeezed her hands in return. "Thank you… you, too." I whispered, feeling all choked up for some reason.

She retrieved her carry-on bag from the storage above us and swiftly walked to the front of the plane.

I often think of my nameless friend and her grandsons and wonder how they are.

Are her hopes and dreams for them coming true? I certainly hope so.

Patent Leather Shoes

by Barbara Emanuelson

In my life, there's an event that left an imprint on me in ways I had no idea would affect my future so profoundly. It would forge the path my life would one day take, though I didn't know it at the time. I learned so much from that golden experience.

It is my belief, in some way, I had an encounter with an angel or with the Lord Himself in the guise of ordinary human beings.

When I was a child, I relished wearing my Sunday best clothes and shoes. There were dainty protocols to be observed in 1959, in the city of Baltimore. It was an era of fashion, polish, city life for my family and me. I loved my black T-strapped patent leather shoes. They were glossy and had real heels, just like grownup shoes. I'd slip them over my lacey socks before donning my petticoat and Polly Flinders dress. I remember staring at them in the mirror as my mother helped me into my spring coat and lacy bonnet. The crowning touch was the hand-stitched white gloves. The miniature white purse completed my outfit.

Off to church our family went, mother and father, children, and my grandmother. I was a bitsy girl of four years old, the third of five children. After church, we went to Sunday brunch at a fine restaurant owned by some friends of my parents. We were doted on, as usual, with our Shirley Temple drinks and extra treats to go with our meal.

When it was time to go, my dad ushered us out of our special round "big family" booth and stepped out onto the sidewalk. The wind seemed to speak as we moved past the tall buildings, whistling through the alleyways and sidewalks. After a block or so, I saw our car.

We were almost to it when a woman approached. I can still see her clutching the tattered sweater around her thin, pink calico dress. She wore a pair of scuffed-up patent leather shoes. Her eyes were dark. In those eyes, there seemed to be a kindness laced with sadness. She glanced over our large family and the shiny black Mercury in front of us. Her brown hair was tied in a loose bun, with escaped tendrils touching her round cheeks as the wind pushed the curls close to her face.

"Excuse me, sir, but can you spare a dime for a crumb of bread?" she asked my father through a shaky voice.

I glanced up at my father, and I saw a crease creep onto his forehead.

He nodded and said, "Of course."

He pulled several dollars from his trouser pocket. He reached over and put it into her outstretched hand, wrapping her fingers around the wad. He didn't say another word, though his gentle blue eyes spoke volumes as he blinked against the sunlight and stark face of poverty. I can still recall the soft expression he wore as he gazed at her and the sound of his breathing as he tried to force back his emotions.

There were tears in the woman's eyes and she gulped before whispering, "Thank you, sir. Oh, thank you so much."

She drew her dingy, white sweater around her as she headed down the alleyway. I remember how she scuttled through the cluttered road as if the wind were sweeping her away. We all watched as she made her way through the narrow road lined with garbage cans and trash. Then, she stopped and turned around, giving us a wave and a smile before hurrying out of sight.

"Who was that, Daddy?" I asked.

"A nice lady," was all he said.

My older sister gasped in the direction of the alleyway and asked, "Where'd she go, Daddy?"

We all stared at the now-empty littered alley. I had quite a shiver, the kind you get before blowing out birthday candles on your cake.

There was a momentary stillness before my mother, father, and grandmother made the Sign of the Cross.

My grandmother murmured, "Lord of the Powers, be with us," in her native Greek language,

When we got in the car, my sister, Michele, asked Dad if we had been around a poor lady. My dad said simply, "Yes."

"Why, Daddy?" Michele asked. "How can she be poor if she has patent leather shoes?"

He didn't reply at first. There was an audible silence as we waited for his response. In deliberate and measured words, he said, "Yes, that is an extremely poor woman. We are fortunate to have more."

I can still feel his velvety voice, etching those words onto my heart, even now. I said, "Because we have a nice house, Easter clothes, and pretty shoes? Are we rich?"

My parents exchanged a grin before my father continued. "Because we have more, we could share with her. I have a good job and we have a nice home. Our bellies are full.

That lady was hungry, so we helped her."

"Oh," I said, and leaned closer to my dad. "Because we should?"

"That's right. You see, God would want us to help her with our blessings. Every time someone poor holds out their hand to us, it's as though Jesus is holding out His hand to us."

My dad glanced at the rear seat and saw our puzzled expressions. He explained, "Jesus said, '…When you do this to the least of my brothers, you do it to me.' That means we treat everyone the way we'd treat Jesus. It means helping if we can and doing it with a happy heart. Everything we have really belongs to Him, comes from Him. So, we're supposed to share. When we do, we show God how much we love him, and it pleases Him."

"Is this God's love?" Michele asked.

My dad nodded and I can still see his shoulders shaking as he wiped his eyes with his starched white monogrammed handkerchief. "It sure is," he said. "For us, and hopefully, for the lady."

Michele glimpsed at me before speaking, scooting herself up close to the front seat. "I hope she can get some new patent leather shoes, Daddy."

I bounced in my seat and replied, "Yep. With straps like ours and pretty heels on them."

Perhaps the Lord Himself had appeared to us that Sunday. Per chance, we were in the company of one of His angels, or merely an ordinary woman in need. I do know this: It was an opportunity to show love. The dignity and generosity my dad gave her has stuck with me as a blueprint for stewardship to God and His people—all people, no matter whom or what walk of life from which they hail.

I have often wondered if it was providence I eventually married a man who would become an Orthodox Christian priest and if that seed planted in my heart so long ago made me choose a man of God. All I know is we share the same feelings and values.

When someone reaches out their hand to us for help—be it for time, treasures, talents, or simply a kind word or two—we try to help and we are always the ones who receive the greater blessing for it.

There are always opportunities coming our way, often when we don't expect them. And… they may just be in the shape of a woman in tattered clothing and scuffed up, worn-out, patent leather shoes.

Chance Meeting on a Busy Street

by Doug Gibson

In 1983, I celebrated my twentieth birthday in Chiclayo, Peru. I was a missionary for The Church of Jesus Christ of Latter-day Saints, also known as Mormons.

Chiclayo was a dusty city then; more so in the "*pueblo jovenes*," semi-squatter settlements with dirt roads and mud-brick homes. In the urban parts of the city, dust was more obscured, competing with concrete.

Missionaries do a lot of tramping through the streets, knocking on doors, but there are other tasks. Nearly forty years ago, a barely out-of-the-teens "gringo" with a white shirt, slacks, and tie was considered essential clergy in Peru, able to advise local ecclesiastical leaders in their sixties.

Imagine facing a Mormon bishop — standing with a shame-faced teen — and being asked to share my wisdom on chastity or morality with young people at a time when my nineteen-year-old self was often sneaking lustful glances at older girls in public school uniforms.

My daily scripture readings were too often invaded by thoughts of whether Larry Holmes was still heavyweight boxing champion or how the California Angels were doing in baseball.

Even though I appreciated my missionary companions they would annoy me at times, and me them, I'm sure. Occasionally, my companion and I were called on to give health blessings to the sick, injured, or those struggling with emotional issues.

These visits were often done in hospitals or care centers. In 1983 third-world Peru, they were cold, brick edifices, often crowded, and retaining the ever-present dust. Sometimes Lizards would scamper across a wall.

When I gave a blessing, my motivation was not to say anything that could go wrong. That fear overrode any inclination to follow spiritual "promptings." To a very old woman slowly dying in a hospice setting, I blessed with the hope of an easy passage to a joyful reunion with those she had known and loved. Afterward, she smiled.

She died two weeks later.

I felt inadequate in this assumed position of spiritual "powerhouse." I had a testimony of what we call the Gospel. I believed I was where God wanted me to be. I was there, showing up, which the cliché says is ninety percent of success. I often felt myself a poseur.

One day, we were walking through the streets on our way to deliver a "*charla*," a Gospel lesson.

We'd been traipsing through dirt streets and knocking on doors. My companion and I narrowly missed being drenched with a large bucket of water thrown from the door by a housewife. She meant no malice. Later, the bucket would be refilled at the community station fifty yards away.

Children playing with old tires circled us as we walked through the dirt roads.

We moved deeper into the city, walking on sidewalks, on streets of concrete, dotted with potholes, the walkways releasing grass and weeds from aged cracks. We passed small restaurants, one touting its barbecued guinea pig and another serving marinated fish. On the other side of the street, there was a pharmacy and a money-trading shop where U.S. dollars were exchanged for *soles*, the Peruvian currency at the time.

Passersby who were used to missionaries, gave us few glances.

Across the busy street, I observed several young adult members of our local congregation. They waved their arms to get our attention.

"Elders, you need to help this man. He needs a blessing," several spoke in unison.

Holding onto our hands, they pulled us to a man sitting on a concrete bench, his head down, hands clasping his knees. As I approached him, his eyes locked on mine.

This is still hard to explain, even today. However, I felt something like power go through me when I saw this person. He was young. His face was infused with deep fear. His eyes greeted me with terror and panic. He clasped his hands on my wrist, not with the gentle squeeze of the ancient I had wished an easy death for. This was a tight, desperate squeeze.

"*Hermano, estoy escupiando sangre,*" he said, telling me, "Brother, I am spitting up blood."

The tone of his voice echoed the palpable fear. His countenance revealed a man appalled, afraid, and bewildered. At this age, we think we are immortal.

Empathy embraced me. I understood I could help this individual, and he could help me. I wasn't to be a spiritual giant. I wasn't one. My role was to help.

I moved behind him. I produced the consecrated oil Mormons use to provide blessings. I placed a drop or two on his head.

Blessings are addressed by name. It did not seem necessary. I called him a brother, one in need. After invoking my ecclesiastical authority, I began the blessing.

With no fear this time of saying the "wrong thing," I felt power and yes, spiritual promptings, when I offered my thoughts to the young man: I don't claim any religious superiority. I am convinced this can happen with anyone, believer or atheist. I do think the power comes from our Creator, however.

I spoke. "I do not know if you will live or die. I testify God understands your fear and confusion. I promise you God will give you strength to endure as Christ endured. If you survive, you will provide comfort and strength to others who endure what you endure and fear as you now. You are loved by your Creator, always."

In our Mormon faith, we are told to listen to a still, small voice. We must heed that voice as it comes from the Holy Ghost. When we embrace truth, we feel a powerful emotion of peace and tranquility in our bosom. I heard the voice and felt the emotion.

The young man's eyes filled with tears. His countenance relaxed; the eyes were no longer haunted. He smiled. He said one word.

"Gracias."

He placed his hands on my shoulders and patted them. I believe he understood my personal doubts and was giving me a needed thumbs-up.

Tears in my eyes, I only nodded. This time, I clasped my hands on his wrists and squeezed.

He walked away.

I never saw him again.

Dressed for Success

by Wendy Toliver

My husband and I were on a business trip in Dallas, Texas and spontaneously decided to go to a club where his cousin was deejaying.

Not long after getting in, a pretty lady in her mid-twenties caught my eye, flashed a friendly, yet shy, smile, and sidled over to our table. She was dressed to be in the spotlight—short skirt, off-shoulder top, high heels. Her hair and makeup, nightclub-heavy and flawless. Still, something about the way she held herself and the way she kept shifting her long-lashed eyes side-to-side, gave me the feeling she was out of her comfort zone.

Perfect. Because I was, too.

I loved going dancing, but I wasn't a typical club-goer. I was about ten years older than most of the people there. I was married. I didn't know anyone there, besides the deejay and my husband. And, my husband never danced, so I knew I'd be dancing alone, in a swarm of strangers.

Lucky for me, this young woman wanted to dance. We hung out the whole night, and I had a great time dancing and talking with her. She kept tugging on my heartstrings—maybe it was a "big sister" or "maternal" chemistry that drew me to her. To this day, what drew *her* to *me* is a mystery.

Later, she confided in me that it was her first time out in public, dressed in women's clothing. She wanted to go someplace by herself, with no bubble of friends to protect her. A place where no one would recognize her. She wanted to see what it felt like to dress in a way that felt more authentic to her than in the masculine clothes she usually wore. The type of clothes generally expected and accepted for a young man to wear. She wanted to spend an evening tuned in to her*self*.

She thanked me for staying with her and also for helping her with her dance moves. When the deejay started putting away his equipment and the bartender stopped serving, she gave me the sweetest hug. I felt like we'd genuinely connected.

Wherever she is now, and whether she decided to keep dressing in women's clothes all the time, occasionally, or never again, I hope she knows how honored I was to have been her friend for a night. I hope she is happy.

And yeah, I hope she found somebody besides me — someone who can actually dance — to help her with those dance moves.

Co-Workers

by Celeste Kuun

In 2009, I worked in Scotland in a luxury hotel in the middle of nowhere. Literally. The nearest town was four miles away.

It was more like a hamlet really, with a convenience shop, pub, tearoom, nursery, and doctor's surgery. To get to the "town," there was a bus that ran twice a day- once in the morning into town and once in the afternoon back to the hotel. Otherwise, you could catch a lift with the post van if he happened to pass your way that day.

When I first saw the hotel, I was in awe. The mansion was built in the Victorian era. Construction was completed around 1857. It is an imposing white sandstone building with a grey slate roof and spire that looked so tall, it seemed to touch the sky. It was built by a rich merchant for his wife. He died before the mansion was completed. His widow went on to live there with her butler until both passed away... in the house. There are many spooky stories about the hotel. Staff were housed in a building at the lower portion of the property, near the road and overlooking the loch.

What I did not bargain on was falling ill two weeks after arriving for work at the hotel. It started as good ol' influenza. I mean, don't all illnesses start out that way? I had the sore throat, achy body, hoarse voice, and the worst headache I have had in my whole entire life. I tried to push through the symptoms and went to work anyway. My manager informed me if I didn't look and feel better by the next morning, I would have to take a sick day. I was touched, thinking he cared for my health, but I later realized I was probably scaring the guests with my sickly pallor and croaky talking.

Sure enough, the next day I felt ten times worse than the night before. I phoned my manager and told him I was taking his advice and staying in bed. I went back to bed and woke up with a splitting headache in the middle of the night. My throat and neck were swollen. Breathing and swallowing was nigh on impossible. Talking was out of the question. And so, unfortunately, was sleeping, due to the headache.

I got up the following morning, called in sick again, got dressed and went to the bus stop to wait for the bus to town. I went to the convenience shop to buy paracetamol and whatever else looked medicinal on their shelves. To soothe my burning throat, I bought ice lollies and rice to cook with lots of salt. I absolutely detest rice, but it was the only food my body could process.

While in town, I came across a co-worker, Natalia, and her boyfriend, Liam. She was from Spain and worked as a bartender. He was Scottish and the sous chef in the main kitchen. They offered me a lift to the hotel, which I accepted, although not graciously because who can be gracious with snot dripping from your nose.

Later, Natalia returned with a bowl of soup and a toasted sandwich. Even though the food went uneaten, I was thankful for the gesture.

The following morning, I developed a rather high fever. When Natalia came to check on me, she was alarmed to see I was more ill. She insisted Liam drive me to the doctor's surgery that afternoon. This was during the swine flu epidemic, where doctors turned away consultations from all but the most ill people.

He saw *me* right away.

Multiple samples were taken: my temperature (which was forty-two degrees Celsius), blood (which was poorly oxygenated), and a urine sample (which showed early signs of kidney failure). Natalia and Liam waited patiently in their car and drove me back to the hotel. Natalia worried over me the whole afternoon, bringing me glasses of water I was unable to drink and reheating yesterday's soup over and over which I still couldn't eat.

Natalia got busy at work over the weekend and into the next week. It was the middle summer after all and tourists were flocking to the hotel and loch. She popped in for visits when she could. In the meantime, the doctor contacted the hotel to tell them I was not to return to work for at least two weeks. Finally, I could put a name to this horrible illness: glandular fever.

I lay in my malaise miasma for a week, all alone, only leaving my bed to shower. At last, there was a break in the constant stream of tourists and Natalia returned to check up on me. She was concerned over how the symptoms were not dissipating. I gave a wan smile as she left for her evening shift.

An hour later, there was a knock on my door. I knew it wasn't Natalia because she usually burst into the room without knocking. I opened up only to find the general manager of the hotel standing there, in his neat designer suit, wearing a deep look of concern on his face.

"Ah, Celeste. Natalia tells me you're feeling poorly," he said.

I nodded my head, quite literally unable to speak due to my swollen throat.

"Well, I guess you had better come with us then," he said.

I thought I was being deported, due to missing as many days as I'd worked. To my surprise, he ordered one of the groundskeepers to drive me to the hospital. Once there, a very attractive doctor peered down my disgusting throat and immediately put me on a steroid drip. Within the hour, the swelling in my throat stopped and I could swallow, breathe freely, and talk again. I was sent home with a course of steroids and antibiotics to complete and a further week of bed rest.

It seemed Natalia had turned up for her shift in floods of tears that evening, claiming I was dying. Her obvious distress prompted Liam to tell the general manager how ill I was, and the general manager came to check up on me.

Sadly, on my last day of bedrest, Natalia burst into my room one last time. She and Liam had been transferred to a hotel in the northern parts of Scotland and they had come to say goodbye.

The kindness of Natalia and Liam saved my life. They had no incentive to help me in any way, beyond the gratification of being thoroughly decent human beings.

Helping Hands

by Dimitria Van Leeuwen

They say opposites attract; maybe that's why I fell in love with Mexico City. It was so different from my hometown of Salt Lake City, so it had my full attention right away.

The softness of the air. The contrast of shiny and new right next to ancient and weathered. The traffic moving like blood through arteries in an organic rush. Painted murals blended with a generous profusion of plants and flowers. Wealth and poverty. Music. Food. Vibrant life. So many beautiful faces, so many different types of people I met there.

It was my third stay in the city, and I walked every morning to a little cafe where a woman named Claudia made me rich and foamy lattes.

On my way there, I smiled and nodded my hello at the security guards and shop keepers I saw each day. It was September, and the jacarandas, which in spring are bursting with purple blossoms covering the sidewalks in a lavender carpet, were now beautiful in a different way, with graceful twisting branches and soft, feathery leaves. I watched shopkeepers sweep their sidewalks and children in bright clean clothes and well-groomed hair, laughing with their grandparents on their way to school.

I wrote in my diary, "Maybe this city will adopt me…"

Late one morning, I returned home after a hot walk around the Colonial Roma neighborhood. I walked up the stairs of the beautiful old house and again up more outside stairs to the little rooftop apartment that I rented. I kicked off my tennis shoes and flopped onto the bed, tired from the heat.

I was idly scrolling through my phone when the shaking started. It took me a second to realize what was happening. My bed knocked into the wall, and a loud, low rumbling sound seemed to come from everywhere. I jumped up, put my feet into some slip-on shoes, grabbed my phone, and opened the door onto the roof.

The protocol most residents follow is to get out of buildings in case they collapsed.

Down the iron stairs attached along the back of the building, I grabbed the railing hard as I moved as fast as I could. I heard a door slam somewhere and glass breaking. Car alarms sounded off all around. Someone screamed. The chaotic rumbling of buildings knocking together and the shifting Earth was omnipresent.

I got out the front door and the rocking of the building caused it to slam shut behind me. I had forgotten to grab my key.

I tried to walk through the diminutive alleyway to get to the street in front of my building, swaying, trying to keep my balance, like I remembered it being in the funhouse as a kid.

Hundreds flooded the street with me. Trees and power lines swayed and shook. There were people everywhere pouring out of nearby buildings, but they were moving calmly and quietly.

One man stood in the street wearing nothing but an overcoat and tennis shoes with no socks. His hair was dripping wet.

I must have seemed overwhelmed because I noticed a man in his sixties near me, trying to catch my eye.

While watching me, he raised and lowered his hands, slowly, in time with his breathing.

"*Calmate.*" He said it so kindly.

I nodded and tried to breathe. The Earth still shook around us.

"*Es muy fuerte,*" he said.

"*Si,*" I agreed. "It *is* strong."

It began to slow down, then it was over. I had never before been unable to count on the very stability of the earth under my feet, and it was a disorienting to feel in that moment that nothing can be trusted. My adrenaline was high, but the fight was over. I had nowhere to go. I'd heard the expression "weak in the knees" before and was now living it. I walked to the cafe next to my place and sat in a chair, not knowing what to do next.

A young woman hurrying down the sidewalk ran up to the waiter who was smoking a cigarette next to me and spoke to him urgently.

"*Perdon,*" I asked her. "I'm sorry, I don't understand…"

"The gas!" she screamed. "There is gas leaking, stop smoking!"

Many were on their cell phones. Everyone seemed calm, but in shock with serious expressions on their faces.

Some people huddled up in quiet tears, comforting each other. Dogs milled about, although I couldn't tell if they were with their owners or not. Some people walked purposefully in one direction or another, occasionally someone ran, but most simply stood there, waiting, not sure where to go or how to get there. I saw a European couple, tourists with backpacks, standing quietly next to each other, watching, unsure, trying to take it all in.

I couldn't understand most of what people around me were saying. I'm sure it was only my impression, but everyone else seemed to have someone to talk to, to connect with. I felt very alone.

Traffic crawled. There were vehicles on every available bit of road. On my right, I could see a parking garage had partially crumbled and there were cars covered in cement and rebar. Strong-looking men began clearing the large white chunks of broken building from the cars.

I was locked out and felt lost, so I decided to walk to my uncle's apartment, about ten blocks away.

As I turned the corner, I saw a four-story metal facade of a building had fallen onto a white convertible that seemed like it had been into the underground parking. An enormous metal grid had fallen onto the driver's seat. The door was open, but there was no one inside.

I gazed up at the building, it appeared like a dollhouse where you can remove the front and look into the house, into people's lives, the floor lamp, the desk covered with papers and a printer, a red office chair with its back to what had been the front wall, the potted plants, opening to the sky.

Another block, I saw water bubbling up from the asphalt in the middle of the street. There was broken glass, tile, and concrete in many places.

Near the park there were many cars waiting to turn into the neighborhood. As one waited, I saw a woman run up to the car and tap on the window. The window was rolled down and she spoke to the driver urgently.

I knew enough Spanish to understand that her daughter was at the school several blocks up the street and she was frantic to get there.

I heard the click of the door unlocking as the driver let her in.

Halfway to my uncle's house, I came upon a collapsed office building. I found out later it had been seven stories, now condensed into unrecognizable debris. There were men along the top searching for signs of life.

I continued along Alvaro Obregon, a beautiful street with many restaurants, hotels, and shops. In the center of the street is a tree-lined lane with benches and fountains. The hospital had evacuated there. Hospital staff and patients filled the lane for a block, some in hospital beds, attached to IVs and other various other machines.

I kept walking. It was hot and I would have loved a glass of water. My tank top strap slid off my shoulder as I continued up the sidewalk. I noticed an older man watching me. When he saw me glance at him, he smiled appreciatively and said in a low, flirtatious accented voice, "Hellooooo."

I couldn't help but let out a laugh, the kind that happens when you've been holding your breath and haven't noticed.

Really? Even in the middle of this insanity?

Fortunately, when I arrived at my uncle's house my family's apartment building was intact. I knocked on their door and there were hugs all around.

Sometime later, I returned home. I hadn't yet reached the host family I was renting from and I was still locked out. So, when I got to my street, I sat on someone's step next to the cafe to think about what to do next.

After about five minutes a young couple and another man came home and saw me on their doorstep. I apologized in my abysmal Spanish and moved aside. The young woman was the owner of the cafe and recognized me. They invited me into their home to wait until I could go home. The single man was named Alejandro and he offered me a beer as we sat in the living room. When he discovered I was staying on the rooftop next door, he volunteered to help get me back in the house.

He went onto his roof, scaled a wall, made his way carefully over a thin aluminum awning and onto my roof. I had not fully closed the door from the outside stairs into the top floor of the house, so he simply went downstairs and opened the door for me. I thanked him profusely and went up to my room to rest.

I talked with the local family I was staying with about the volunteer efforts underway. Many buildings were too damaged for the occupants to return. So many were in need of essentials and so supply hubs had sprung up around the city.

In the days to follow, I saw handmade signs, posting encouragement and love. Cafes even offered free coffee for volunteers.

Sadly, the funeral home offered free services for those killed in the quake.

The power was still out in many places, so people around the city with motorcycles and scooters drove to collapsed building sites and parked strategically so their headlights shone on the volunteers digging through the rubble.

Donations of food, water, medical supplies, and toiletries were dropped off at various spots around the edge of the park where they were separated and categorized, then handed along the corresponding line (one for water, one for toilet paper, etc.) and put in centralized, coherent piles. Packages were compiled with some of each necessity. Volunteers drove those to the areas where they were most urgently needed.

There seemed to be no authority in charge, only passionate, intelligent people, learning as they went.

It was after nine by now and I found a place in a long double line of people passing supplies. Donations were being taken from people pulling up to the outer rim of the park, then gathered in a main central location.

Our line was organizing the water.

At first, I felt out of place, but somehow, I was also sure this was exactly where I needed to be. I silently waited to be handed jugs or packages of bottled water. We worked fast and steadily.

Sometimes the person handing off the package would say *"pesado"* if it was particularly heavy. Several times, the man to my left tried to bypass me and hand heavy packages to the young man on my right, but I said, "No, here," and held out my arms.

That night, I had incredible strength and endurance. After four hours, I was tired, but I still felt alert and able.

We sweated profusely in the humid air and my hands and clothes were dusty. My naturally wavy hair was a frizzy mess and I have never cared less in my life.

As the man handed me one package after another, moving as fast as possible, but also always aware, considerate of me, we were constantly in contact, hands and arms touching, checking in with each other.

"Do you have it?"

"Yes, I'm ready."

I turned and repeated the process with the young man next in line. Almost an intimate contact, but a rhythm and an energy built up. We had an understanding and knowing, a trust of the other. With each hour that passed, I felt an enormous respect and affection building up within me for these strangers. I truly understood what it means when people say we are all brothers and sisters. In this moment, I belonged fully.

We paused while waiting for more supplies. The young man smiled at me shyly and I smiled back.

"Where are you from?" he asked in a heavily-accented English. I explained I was vacationing here, although it seemed like less than the full truth.

His name was Pablo, and he seemed a bit shell-shocked though he was working hard, thinking quickly, willing and determined. Once he stopped for a moment to look around. "This is just crazy. This is so messed up."

And, the look of shock, of loss, of being lost, would overtake him for a moment, then would make a decisive return of attention to the work at hand.

Whenever there was a break, we talked more. Mostly about the events of the day. He was a student and told me about his school. I told him about Salt Lake City.

Around one a.m., Pablo's phone buzzed. He read over the message and then looked up from his phone. "Another building just collapsed close to here. I should go to see if I can help."

Our eyes met. "Okay. Good luck."

He turned to leave, but then stopped and gazed at me earnestly, briefly, "Thank you for helping us."

"Of course!" was all I could answer. However, what was in my heart was, "It's been an honor to work alongside you."

That night, there was no me or them… only us.

I wanted to say thank you, too. To everyone whose path I'd crossed that day. For the privilege and blessing of feeling a part of so much love.

The All-Weather Ladies Picnic Club

by Drienie Hattingh

It was a stunningly beautiful, yet freezing, blue-sky-Minnesota day in late November.

I gazed out of my window at Cascade Lodge on the North Shore of Minnesota. Lake Superior filled the view from my window.

The lake was not frozen yet. It was a deep azure blue and, even after having lived in Minnesota for eight years, and even after spending countless times at this, my all-time favorite place, I was still stunned by the size of the biggest fresh water lake in the world. Peering over it to the horizon, there seemed to be no end to it. It was like an ocean. It was almost impossible, looking at the horizon, to determine where the sky ended, and the lake began.

I was having an amazing time. It was day two of my five-day vacation, a birthday gift from my darling, thoughtful husband. He told me, "I reserved a room for you at Cascade Lodge."

I gasped hearing this. "What do you mean? I cannot just leave. Who will get Yolandi to school? Who will help with her homework? Who will get Brenda to ballet? Who will get Eugene to college? Who will feed all of you?"

These rapid thoughts made my heart flip as I envisioned such an amazing possibility, but Johan did not think it all through. There was no way he and our three children could get along without me.

As it happened, he had everything planned.

"This is your birthday gift. I want you to have a break from all of *this*..." He spread his arms out wide. "I want you to forget about everything, even forget about *us*... and go and stay at Cascade Lodge and enjoy your most favorite place in the world."

I stared at him in shock. "I cannot go on my own. You must come with me. We cannot just go... we can plan it... arrange for the children to stay with someone and we can go—"

"No! I have to work, and you need a break *now*, not later. You are exhausted."

I stood in our kitchen, holding the lasagna from the oven with my mitts. He stood in the doorway, leaning against the door frame, drinking a cup of coffee. He was so handsome. I felt the roasting pan's heat coming through the mittens and hurriedly put it down on the counter.

Johan was right about me being exhausted. I was close to a complete burn out. The day before I felt like screaming and not stopping when I tried to convince one of our children's principals about what I saw as an injustice at a PTA meeting. The argument went on and on and because of it I was late taking Brenda to her ballet practice in Minneapolis. I rushed home, knowing we will now be in peak traffic all the way to Minneapolis.

After getting home, I shoved the pork roast into the oven and set the timer for three hours—just in time for dinner. I grabbed the sandwiches I had made for my daughters so they could eat during the ride.

Yolandi and Brenda were already waiting in our vehicle when I got in with Yolandi's homework which she would do while Brenda did ballet. Sitting in the peak hour traffic and crossing the mighty Mississippi on the way to Minneapolis, I felt the migraine coming. Perhaps my doctor was right… It might be the beginning of menopause. The migraine peaked when I ran into the building, with Brenda and Yolandi in tow, where I had to man the ballet welcome table, as I did every afternoon.

That night, when Johan got home, I put on a smile. I did not share all my problems with him, knowing he was also tired after visiting Credit Unions (his job) all day long. But… yes, I had to agree with my husband, I was exhausted.

Johan continued, "I want you to go and relax and do stuff you love without worrying about anything. You never have time for *your* stuff. You are too busy with everyone else. You can go on long walks in the snow, go cross-country skiing, read, go on long drives… and *Relaaaaaax*."

He continued with a smile. "Brenda has a break from ballet this week. She can help with meals and I will take Yolandi to school and Brenda can be here in the afternoons. I can help Yolandi with homework and get Eugene to college. The house will survive without you cleaning it for five days. It is all planned."

"It sounds amazing, but I do not know…" I mumbled.

He put his arms around me and said, "You need a break."

So, there I was, at Cascade Lodge, and it was heavenly. Five days to do what I wanted.

Something weirdly wonderful… when I checked into the lodge the previous day, the manager told me, "You will be the only person here for the whole week. Just remember, I lock up at five p.m. Whenever you leave, make sure the front door is locked."

"All alone, really?" I exclaimed. "How wonderful!"

He laughed when I smiled ear to ear. "You can choose any room in the lodge."

I was like a kid in a candy store when I walked through the lodge, savoring every room. Of course, I chose the one with the most beautiful view over the lake.

It was like a dream come true, staying in this lodge, in a winter-wonderland all on my own.

On this lovely day, it was still early; the manager had not arrived yet. I shuffled down the stairs, marveling over how I was completely alone. My house in Woodbury, Minnesota and my daily responsibilities seemed a world away.

I slipped on my boots, coat, hat, and gloves I'd left in the entrance hall the previous night. I opened up and…

Fresh snow!

Overjoyed, I realized I could go cross-country skiing the next day in fresh snow. I drove to the closest town, Grand Marais, for breakfast at my favorite restaurant, Blue Water Café. As I walked into the restaurant, a group of old-timers greeted me.

"Oh, you are back," one man said.

Puzzlement must have crossed my face until I remembered seeing the man here yesterday. "Yes, I love eating here."

"Come join us," he said and got up and pulled a chair out.

I smiled, thinking how strange it would be in the big city if a stranger asked you to join them but, here on the North Shore, it was fine.

After a lovely breakfast, I said "see you later" to my new friends, who I would be seeing every morning for the rest of the week. When I wanted to pay at the till, the girl told me someone already paid my bill. I glanced over at the table and they all smiled and nodded at me.

"Thank you," I said with a laugh.

My next stop was at Gooseberry Falls. I wanted to go on a long hike through the forest, in the snow. After looking at the partly frozen falls, I started my walk, inhaling deeply, and savoring the cool air enhanced by pine scent. It had started to snow, and it was truly a winter-wonderland. Snow drifted down in huge flakes and settled all around me on the tall pine trees.

I came around a corner on the trail and there, between the snow-covered pines, was a group of ladies, sitting around a picnic table. By the looks of it, they were having a picnic. What a beautiful picture they made. Eight elderly ladies, in brightly colored coats, hats and scarves, with snow falling down on them. Looked like a snow globe. Their chatter and laughter filled the cold snowy morning.

One lady saw me and said something. Everyone turned to me. "Hi," one of them called out, "Come and join us."

The other ladies called out "Good morning."

I answered their greeting and one of the ladies shifted over and made space for me.

"Coffee?" the lady across from me asked.

I gladly accepted the warm-up.

"What are you doing here? Where are you from?"

"I live in Woodbury, close to St. Paul. My husband gave me a week off," I said with a smile. "He said I needed a break from everyday life."

They all gasped and some exclaimed, "How wonderful!" and "You have a keeper!" and "You have a wonderful husband!"

"I hear an accent, are you from England?" one lady asked.

Another lady said, "No… I'm guessing you're from Australia, or, maybe New Zealand?"

"I'm from South Africa." I said, with a laugh.

"Really," she exclaimed. "That must have been a change coming from a hot climate to our freezing one."

Another woman asked, "How did you adapt to the freezing winters here?"

I laughed, "Well, actually winter is our favorite season here. We love the snow and all the winter activities, cross-country skiing… even ice-fishing. My husband and I decided to embrace everything in our new country… freezing winters, culture, and all."

I smiled, "we mostly did that for our three children, to help them fit in. And," I said, "we just love having white Christmases."

The women smiled and one said, "Good for you."

I soon learned these ladies had a mid-morning breakfast get-together, every Tuesday, regardless of the weather. Come snow or rain, they met there every

Tuesday, at eleven o'clock. They have been doing it ever since they met each other when they dropped their children off at school for the very first time. After they dropped their children off at school, they met.

A lady next to me said, "You know, at first, it was a getaway from everyday life for me, but later, it became more. We started sharing whatever happened in the previous week, the good and the bad."

The women laughingly shared a bit of their lives with me. Some had difficult times and some even lost their husbands and some had battled severe illnesses. But, they never missed a Tuesday morning. It was a time when they were rejuvenated. A time they shared whatever ailed them or their loved ones at the time, and they gave each other love and support. They were there for each other through it all, for the last forty years or so, right up to when they were all empty nesters and stopped working. Right from when they were young wives and mothers, right up to now, they always left, feeling better and ready to take on the new week.

I realized they had weathered a lot during their lives, but they somehow came through it with hope, faith, love, and by being there for each other. I felt fortunate to have met them and decided to practice some of what I learned from them... mainly to take things easier and appreciate what I have, not sweating the small stuff.

I left the happy group of women with smiles and good wishes and carried on with my walk through the snowy woods.

***

That encounter with the group of strangers changed me in that I realized my life was too busy, too complicated. I wanted to have what those ladies had.

When they were about my age, they made a choice to take time to relax, to meet with each other every Tuesday. To visit and take stock. They recharged for the week ahead. It took a load off their shoulders by sharing their problems with each other. It was not too late for me to make changes and follow their example.

I decided to cut back on the committees I served on. I stopped being the crazy mother who rushed from one place to another. Suddenly, I was more relaxed during those long drives to and from Minneapolis for ballet. I started to enjoy it. My daughters shared what happened to them that day at school. The times with my daughters and son, on the way to ballet, hockey, and to college, was the perfect time to talk and share.

And soon, I greeted Johan with a real smile, not a fake one, when he came home from a long day at work. When we sat down to dinner, we enjoyed each other's company and laughed and joked. It really was all up to me. If I was happy and relaxed, so would my family be.

I also realized, after spending the short time with those ladies, admiring their beautiful life-long friendships, I had been neglecting my own friends. I wanted my friends to be forever friends, like those women in the All-Weather Ladies Picnic Club.

I had to spend more time with them.

And I did.

The Winter Angel

By Karen Jelinek

It was right before Thanksgiving 2012 when my mom and I headed up to the cabin for the holiday weekend. She had broken her wrist in October, so I drove my 2001 Ford Focus with her in the passenger seat. The rest of the car was full of our overnight gear and food.

My parents had purchased the cabin in September, so we didn't have furniture, clothes, or much of anything stored up there yet.

Heading North on Wisconsin Highway 35 just past Frederic, we hit an especially icy patch and began sliding out of control. I freaked out and started praying, "Oh God, oh God…" over and over, hoping He would hear and help keep us safe.

We spun into the oncoming lane and down into the snowy ditch. Luckily, there was no one else coming the opposite direction at that moment or else things could have been way worse.

The snow was up to the bottom of the car and there was no way we were going to get out of there without a tow. We called my dad and brother, who happened to already be at the cabin, which was less than ten minutes away. Dad hopped in his Saturn to come find us, not that he would have been able to do much once he got to us.

In the meantime, a hunter in a huge pickup truck found a service road on the other side of the ditch and came to see if we were okay and needed help. Ever so grateful, I explained what had happened.

He dug with his bare hands in the snow at the back of my car until he was able to reach the axle. He then took a hook and a rope attached to his pickup and connected the two vehicles. With some work, he ended up pulling my car out of the ditch and onto the service road.

We were so thankful and tried to pay him for his time, effort, and kindness. However, he would not take it.

"I just happened to be here at the right time to help you out," he said. "Perhaps you could do the same if you come across someone in need one day."

By the time my dad found where we had spun off the road, we were out of the ditch and the hunter was gone.

Every time I drive by the spot, I think of what happened and how our Winter Angel came to our rescue.

Is he still out there saving others?

The Mother's Day Moose

by Penny M. Ogle

I have found when you lose someone, things that meant the most to them often have a new meaning for you. A butterfly fluttering over my head brings my dear mother close to my heart. I hear a familiar saying and memories of my college "Chum Buddy" come rushing to the forefront of my conscious thought.

However, for those of us who have endured the loss of a precious child, you never know what will trigger a memory, a smile or… tears.

We lost our adult son suddenly and tragically. No chance to say goodbye. No chance to create a suit of armor to protect against the sad triggers or find the images that will generate the happy memories.

Over the past few years, I discovered a few special things which our son was passionate about. He cared for nature and the environment. He majored in Native American Cultures and minored in Alternative Technology. He hugged the Redwoods, and, in the end, he lived on the reservation; helping his Native American friends plant crops and, using the skills he learned in college, enhance their lives.

In his journal, I read about his feeling of renewed hope when he found the feather of a Blue Heron. And his awe when a Bull Moose appeared, from what seemed like nowhere, wandering through his crude campsite and bedding down for the night.

These thoughts were the beginning of my protective suit of armor.

Like his father, Derek was born on Mother's Day. His birthday was always a special celebration. It was a family time with all four children joining in to create a fun, happy party. It was on a Mother's Day I found my armor cracking and all at once my vulnerability became my reality.

When the fragile shell holding you together... cracks... your guts come spilling out. Without warning, you are crying and sobbing. No matter what you tell yourself... No matter how hard you hold your breath or try to think about happier times, nothing will stop the tide... nothing will end the tears...nothing will change the reality that you will never hug your child again... nothing.

The vessel was empty.

That was how I found myself that Mother's Day morning... alone, and empty, standing forlornly in my house staring blankly out my living room window. We lived in a ski resort on the edge of a golf course. It was a sunny day, and the surrounding mountains should have brought me comfort and peace. Instead, I could not stop the tears or think a single happy thought.

I paced around the room touching the remnants of him. The framed football jersey, his graduation picture, an album of baby pictures... the red blown glass plate etched with his name and the dates of his birth and death staring at me... an undeniable proof of the horrible reality.

We had climbed a mountain to a favorite spot where he and his brother had last hiked. We poured his ashes into the plate and offered it up for the wind to scatter him around the meadow.

The window was open, and I could hear golfers on the course laughing and challenging each other. Staring out the window, I began to question what I was seeing. At first, I thought it was another golf cart. I moved to get a better view and wiped my eyes to be sure. What looked like a golf cart, actually had a rack on its head.

As I watched through tear-soaked eyes, a moose was sauntering from the golf course and heading down the street toward our house. It kept coming, gradually moving in my direction.

I hadn't realized I had stopped crying and could almost feel a smile creeping into my face. I thought for sure the moose would turn and run; but it kept coming, crossing the street, and walking through the auxiliary parking space in front of our office window. Was it my imagination or was he actually peering into the window? His head was cocked almost as if to say, "Stop crying, Mom. You will be okay."

I stood stock still for fear any movement would spook him and he would run away.

When he did move, he continued across our side yard and headed to the garden in the back. I came alive and rushed to the deck to see where he was headed, but I couldn't see him anywhere. I ran to the edge of our property and glanced both ways… nothing. I ran to the front yard and looked up and down the street… nothing. Did he turn and go back to the course… nothing. There was no sign of the moose. Where could he have gone? How could he have disappeared as suddenly as he had appeared? I went out on the lawn and saw his hoof prints through the yard and as I did, I noticed they got fainter and fainter until… they vanished.

I have seen other moose in our neighborhood. None have come close enough to appear to stare in my window. None have stayed in any one spot or strolled around our house before disappearing.

The Mother's Day Moose was a mystery.

He came when I most needed him and stayed until I had regained my sense of self. He calmed me and helped me believe our son was with me. I will always have a place in my heart for a lonely moose. I will smile when I see him and, at the risk of sounding a bit crazy, I will whisper greetings to Derek and remind him I love him… totally.

They Changed My Life

by Alex Montanez

It was a busy night at the restaurant; servers dashing to and fro. Customers lined up at the door waiting for a seat. No one knew of the feelings of lonesomeness I was experiencing.

You see, even surrounded by people, one can feel all alone and that's how I felt that night.

There was no time to be feeling sorry for myself. I had guests to attend to. As I gazed through my list, I came across a woman's name and called it out. I saw a hand go up and I went over to meet the two elderly ladies who sized me up me with kind eyes. I welcomed them and asked if they would follow me to their table.

Once they were seated; I gave them their menus and told our guests I would be right back.

When I returned, I began to explain my featured entrees and one of the ladies politely interrupted me.

She said, "May I tell you something?"

"Sure."

She said they had been watching me as I tended to the other tables and thought I was courteous and welcoming to all the people.

I thanked her and was about to tell them about our specials when she said a strange thing.

"It seemed as though we were walking on Holy Ground as we entered the restaurant."

Needless to say, I was stunned by this comment. I felt strange, as if electricity coursed throughout my body. I smiled nevertheless and tried again to continue before she interrupted me.

" —I want you to know this is your church."

Now, I was even more puzzled and intrigued. All I could say was "thank you" and managed to finish telling them about the specials for the evening.

As I continued my duties; everything started to become clear to me. Some months earlier, I resigned from the position of associate pastor of my local church because of commitments to our new family restaurant. I couldn't handle it all. When I resigned, I had a growing feeling of regret. The restaurant was becoming quite popular, but I had the nagging feeling I was letting God down because of the restaurant. In fact, I was beginning to feel deeply saddened about my personal relationship with God and wondered if I made a huge mistake in resigning.

But that night, when these wonderful women entered my restaurant and said the things they said, it changed my life forever. I knew God had not forgotten me and He loved me more than I could ever imagine. I had a feeling He might even be proud of me.

He sent those ladies with a message, telling me to not regret what I did. I could worship God wherever I was, even in my restaurant. Wait… wasn't that what the sweet lady told me?

"… this is your church."

They enjoyed their dinner and thanked me for being so kind.

I never saw them again.

The Comforting Cardinals

by Barbara Emanuelson

Being a pastor's wife is like being an auxiliary officer in God's military. It means uprooting the family and setting down some roots in whatever place you are called to live. Sometimes you get a choice and sometimes you don't. But you do it, nevertheless.

This is never an easy thing to do. It's always hard leaving one place and going to live in another. You leave so much behind, including a house you love, shops and restaurants you frequent, and the friends and neighbors who've become like family to you.

So, it's no surprise most of us become adaptable, especially when we put our trust in providence.

At times of great need and loneliness, God sends me comfort. It may be in the form of a good person's help or a friendly gesture by a stranger. And it may just be a bird with a musical chirp and profusions of red and black appearing on my windowsill. Such a bird is the happy cardinal. They always seem to come to me when I'm longing for a loved one who has passed from this life onto the next.

One such day, it was October 2002 and we'd just moved to Utah. I knew absolutely no one there. It was not easy to move from my comfortable, forested surroundings in Charlottesville, Virginia to the great desert state of Utah. I grew up in Virginia, loving the tidal areas, rolling hills, and lush, deciduous forests throughout. They have old round mountains I refer to as the "friendly" mountains. I actually gave them the name after I saw the mountains in Utah.

I'll never forget my first glimpse of the giant, monstrous, and imposing Ben Lomond Mountain. It loomed over me as I drove up the street to my new home after a three-day journey from east to west. I couldn't help but gasp because it almost seemed like the mountain would swallow me up. The colors in this strange land were brown and more browns, and I felt the vacuous openness of this new area I'd have to learn to call "home."

What kind of place is *this, anyway?*

Early one morning, I stared out my kitchen window as I gazed up and up and up at the mountain which was less than a mile from my back deck. My husband was at church and the girls were at school. I was alone in the house for the first time since we'd gotten there. It seemed as if the sun was shining more brightly than I could remember ever having seen.

Despite the clear sky and fluffy white clouds, I was not a happy person in my new surroundings.

"What have you done to me, Jon Emanuelson?" I growled out as I unpacked the glasses. "How could you bring the kids and me to live in this desert? Oh, God, I'm all alone here! Oh, Lord, can you even hear me?" I screamed out loud.

For the first time since we'd gotten the news of our transfer from Virginia, I allowed myself to cry. Once I let loose the flood of tears, I couldn't seem to stop. "I might as well be in another galaxy," I said, as though someone could hear me. "Yeah...beam me up, Scotty," I snapped with a bite in my tone.

And then, for some inexplicable reason, I thought of my grandmother who'd been gone from us eight years now. "God, how I wish Yiayia was still alive and here with me. She'd know what to do. She could make this all better. She'd tell me why this was a good thing. Oh, Yiayia. I hate this place." I continued weeping as I finished the glasses.

At long last, the tears subsided, and my eyes found the big box labelled "dishes." I set about unpacking them in the silent house, unwrapping each dish one-by-one, as each layer exposed the next.

After yanking out the remaining paper, I saw something like a parcel at the bottom of the box. It appeared to have been lovingly placed there. I bent to lift it and put it right onto the countertop. I began peeling the many layers of paper back. For some reason, I felt at peace and reconciliation covered me like a warm blanket.

A hug from Yiayia, I thought.

I felt the muscles in my face make their way into a smile, and it felt like relief washing over me. There was a quiet stillness in the room with the only sounds being crackling of paper and my own sighs.

I heard a *tap-tap-tapping* at the window over the sink. At first, I ignored it as I continued with my task.

However, the pitter-patter grew louder and louder. Something was an insistence for attention, so I spun around toward the window.

Sitting outside on the brick of the windowsill was a beautiful she-cardinal. Her eyes met mine and she tilted her head as though she greeted me. I had to laugh.

Are they even indigenous to this state?

I pivoted to the parcel on my countertop, ripping at the last layer. To my astonishment, it was the hand-crocheted tablecloth my Yiayia made when I got engaged. It was her own pattern with Byzantine crosses on it.

Happy tears came at that moment. I picked it up and held it to my face. There was still a hint of the *L'Aire du Temps* perfume my grandmother always had loved.

I moved to the sink and gazed outside. The cardinal was still there and began pecking once again. It stopped when I got close and blinked once… and then again.

"Thank you, Yiayia," I whispered.

As though the bird understood, she bowed her head. And then with a flash she flew away.

My dark mood was gone now and at once I noticed how lovely Utah was. It was no wonder our town was named Pleasant View. The sky had the truest blue I'd ever seen and the grand mountain in my back yard greeted me like a big hug. I noticed all the different greens of the plants mixed in with the brown earth. I knew this was a place I could call home.

Every time we've gone to a different town in another state, cardinals make their way to me. They seem to be harbingers of all that is good in a new place; a reminder I'm *not* alone. To me, they are messengers sent to tell me I'll be fine and I'll make it through. More than once, a cardinal has come to me when I thought of my grandmother.

And, every single time, I feel the warmth of the red feathers and friendly flap of their wings, like one of Yiayia's great, big hugs.

I breathe in the air of my new home and feel it fill me. I am at peace.

What Mothers Know

by Sherry Wallwork

As mothers, we imagine our children's deaths a million times. We envision them dashing in front of speeding vehicles, falling into campfires, or slipping off rocks into rushing rivers. We even imagine ourselves backing over them in the driveway,

We dread daily their dismemberment, disability, and. God forbid, their death. We say we can't imagine it, but we do. We do it so we can keep them alive.

We don't speak it aloud, we seldom even dare think it, but from the moment they are born, the truth is on our heart like an unrelenting shadow. Our beloved child could die.

And we know if they die, so will we.

So, we stuff them into impenetrable snow suits and indestructible car seats. We slather them in sunscreen, SPF 1000 or higher if we can get it. We insist on seat belts and check on the oil and air bags. We stuff flashlights, pepper spray, and spare change into their purses and backpacks.

We teach them to always look twice before they cross, never run in parking lots, and never, ever speak to strangers. We teach them to swim sideways out of a rip tide, to steer into a skid, and not to touch the brakes when sliding on ice. We teach them not to stand too close to the edge and a million other things designed solely to keep them alive.

Yet, despite all our imagining and preventative efforts, despite all our planning and instructing, our insisting and reminding, we know, though we never, never, ever say it, that it may not be enough.

***

The waiting room of the Delvine County Sheriff's Office was not crowded. Only a couple of folks waiting to see their parole officers, and a young woman I didn't notice at first because she was small, faded, and tucked into the corner by the water fountain. We were each waiting for our numbers to be called.

As a single mother of four, I was not accustomed to hanging out in correctional facilities. I was a bit on edge due to a marginally guilty conscience, (who doesn't get nervous when a police car pulls up behind them at a stop light?) and the fact everyone within my immediate line of sight was either a criminal (I supposed) or packing a gun.

I was there to sell to the Sheriff's Public Relations Department a fabulous, self-contained, easy-to-assemble trade show display. A ten-by-eight Skyline Mirage with a pop-up frame, black fabric panels, and a traveling case on wheels. Naturally, the traveling case could double as a podium. They were expecting a demonstration.

The truth was, I had no idea what I was doing. The stakes were high. I had picked the display up for twenty-five dollars at a public surplus auction and listed it on eBay for two hundred and fifty. My kids needed school clothes and I had expected a quick, anonymous sale with an easy ship. Instead, I got a call from the Sheriff's Office.

When the number popped up on the caller ID, I immediately assumed my arrest was imminent. Though not a hardened criminal, I *am* a mother and aware of possible disaster lurking around every corner. Since I supplemented our family income by buying and selling used and discarded items purchased at lost freight auctions, I wondered: *Did I purchase a stolen item? Has the IRS asked them to check on my quarterlies?*

However, as it turned out, the sheriffs were simply shopping. They were headed to their annual conference and convention in Tampa and needed a proper display.

Perched on the rock-hard plastic of my waiting room chair, I was unhappily feeling the contents of my stomach and wishing desperately I'd skipped the fried egg sandwich… or at least the extra mayo.

Ugg. Nerves.

I smoothed my skirt, checking for lint (always a problem, as the only color I wear under pressure is lint-loving black, due to rumors of it being magically slimming.) Inside my brain, I tried desperately to recall and retain the various vital points of my carefully crafted presentation:

Easy to Assemble, Self-Contained… No! Self-Contained first, and then… what were those other three?

I was spiraling.

In an attempt to calm myself, I closed my eyes and tried some yoga breathing. I pictured myself gracefully assembling the pop-up frame and easily attaching the black fabric panels. Beautifully curved, perfectly smooth. Sighs of admiration from the officers.

See? Breathe. You've got this.

But then, my mutinous imagination returned to the audience. A dozen uniformed officers, arms folded, and guns on hips. Frowns. The pop-up collapsing, black panels sliding awkwardly to the floor, or the display in disarray. I imagined being escorted hastily out of the building to cries of being a shyster.

Aaaughhh! This isn't helping.

I opened my eyes and glanced around, seeking distraction from the panic my all too vivid imagination instigated.

The waiting room was now empty except for me and the young woman, who hadn't moved. Her head was bowed, so I rather shamelessly, examined her. She wore a tidy, but faded, floral dress, pale blue pumps crossed at the ankles, and her hands clasped loosely in her lap. No jewelry, nothing extra, but perfectly neat, carefully put together, and completely self-contained. I couldn't imagine what could have landed such a quiet, ordinary, unassuming woman in the Delvine County Sheriff's Office on a Friday afternoon.

She began to cry. Buckets. Torrents. Like an Arizona monsoon. Really, giant, heaving sobs, and sucking in breath in between. I did not know what to do.

I looked down at my feet. I checked my trade show travel case. I opened my purse and searched for a tissue. The clerk behind the glass was typing. I listened and I waited for a slowing of sobs. I gave up and nervously clutched my purse in one hand and a small pack of funeral tissues, I crossed the floor and sat next to the woman. Her face was buried in her hands, so I waited.

She finally came up for air. I could see from her face she was used to this kind of sorrow. Her eyes were not merely swollen, but sunken and highlighted with the dark circles, the trademarks of lack of care, lack of sleep, lack of proper eating. I held out the tissue, tentatively, not sure if it was the right thing to do.

I wasn't prepared for her smile, so lovely it took me off guard. It was so much more than a smile. Courage, shining strength, and resilience showed through the sodden, swollen face. With that, she reached out to me, a stranger, as if we were the oldest of friends. She thanked me kindly and took the whole package of tissues.

It took a minute of wiping, dabbing, and blowing, along with oxygen replenishing catches of breath, and a hiccup or two before she could speak.

So, I waited. I refused to start with "Are you okay?" She obviously wasn't. But I didn't know how else to break the ice.

I watched as she worried at the soggy and disintegrated tissue in her hand. She lifted her face to me and barely got out, "I'm sorry.

"Oh, don't worry. It's fine. We all have these days."

She sniffed and said, "I'm just very sad today.

I wasn't sure I should ask, but her smile said go ahead, so I did. "Why are you so sad?"

Her name was Ellie and she had come to the sheriff's office to collect her little boy's swimming trunks. Her six-year-old son, Aidan James (named after Ellie's father), had died one year ago today, drowning in a small pond on their neighbor's property. The sheriff had collected the swimming trunks as evidence. Ellie had been waiting for this day all year. She said she counted the days by marking on her calendar.

They were dinosaur trunks. "He loved dinosaurs. He wanted dinosaurs on everything. He loved them so much," she said, wistfully. Of course, my own mother's heart cracked into a million pieces. I stopped wondering what was the right thing to do and I wrapped poor Ellie in my arms.

We both cried like babies; no longer strangers.

I asked her to tell me about her little boy and she did, in great detail.

Aidan James was a lovely little fellow. Dark, dusty curls, wide hazel eyes, and hands that were always grubby. He was forever digging bunkers in their backyard. Their border collie, Jack, was his constant companion, and often helped him dig and bury. Action figures, army men, bags of Legos, dozens of dinosaurs. Aidan hoped--indeed, he counted on--the dinosaurs raising themselves up from the ground where he'd buried them, like peas in the garden, only much larger. He had hoped it would happen in the middle of the night and he would be startled awake by the brontosaurus knocking at his window on the second story, hopefully on a night with a very bright moon.

"Now, he is gone," Ellie said. "The dinosaurs and army men remain. I do not know what to do about it. Any of it."

I let her talk. It seemed the right thing to do.

"Most mornings, I forget how to get up. And when I get do, I do not know what I should do." She dabbed at tears again. "If I do think of something to do, perhaps clean the kitchen, or make myself a sandwich, I'm not one hundred percent sure how to go about it."

I told her she was the bravest person I had ever met, and that I would think of her often. She held both my hands and made me promise to never take my children's lives for granted, to count every moment with them as a gift, and to tell them each day how much I loved them.

So, I did, and so I do.

The clerk called my number. "One minute, please," I said. I hugged Ellie and we cried as mothers who only cared about their babies. When one mother has lost their child, there is no complete comfort. Just a reverent acknowledgement of the unbearable sorrow that must be born and the sacredness of it. I will always stand in awe of the unbelievable courage it takes to live in the face of such a loss.

I don't remember even one moment of my presentation to the sheriff's committee that day, but I have never forgotten—nor will I ever forget—this brief encounter with Ellie and her Aidan James.

We Were the Angels

by Mary Pettersen

It was early on a Sunday morning. We were headed to Crane Lake after a graduation party on Saturday. Just past North Branch on I-35, something ran toward us on the freeway.

Was it a dog? Yes!

Since there was virtually no traffic, we stopped on the shoulder. The dog ran up to our truck. A hunting dog. What was he doing on the freeway? Because we had Ben, our own Golden Retriever with us, we were hesitant to let this dog into our vehicle. However, we couldn't leave him on the freeway. My husband approached him slowly and opened the back door.

He jumped right in.

"Now what?" I asked.

We saw he had a collar with a phone number on it. Keep in mind, this was back in the days before everyone had cell phones, so we had to find somewhere to call. We drove to the next exit and went to the first place of business which was a small restaurant.

We called the number from a pay phone and a woman answered in an anxious voice. "Hullo…"

"Hi, this is Mary Pettersen. We picked up your dog on the freeway."

"Oh! Thank goodness. We've been so worried." I could hear the total relief in her voice. "My husband was in an accident early this morning and is okay, but in all the excitement, our dog got out of the truck and ran away from the scene of the accident. We have been looking for him everywhere. Thank you so much."

"I'm so glad your number was on his collar," I said.

"Thank you so much," she said again. "My daughter and I will be right over to pick our dog up."

It wasn't ten minutes later when a little girl jumped out of their car.

"Star," she yelled as she ran to the dog. He yapped and jumped up on her, licking her face over and over.

The little girl's mother came to us. "I do not know

how to thank you." She said, smiling at the happy scene in front of her.

The little girl looked up at us, beaming, her arms wrapped around her beloved dog. "God sent you to find Star! You are angels."

That day… I think we were.

The Freedom Fighters

by Terry Clancy

I grew up in Geneva, Switzerland, and returned to the United States in 1972 at the age of fifteen. My two brothers and I always wanted to go back and visit our friends from school. I graduated from high school in 1975. My older brother Tim and I, we are a year apart in age and shared a number of the same friends. We decided we would return to Geneva and attend our friends' graduation ceremony at the Ecole Internationale de Geneve. We took our younger brother, Kevin, along for the ride.

We decided the best thing to do would be to backpack through Europe for six weeks using first class Eurail passes and use Geneva as a base.

We lived in Bellevue, Washington at the time. We bought bus tickets to Vancouver, British Columbia, and caught a charter flight to Amsterdam. Once we landed in The Netherlands', we hopped a train to Geneva.

The following six weeks were amazing. We would hop a train at around eight at night, sleep in our first-class compartment, and get off at eight a.m. and explore the cities for the day.

We attended our friends' graduation ceremony in Geneva. Everyone wore their countries' native dress to accept their diplomas.

At the end of the six weeks, it was time to return home. We had an early flight to Vancouver, so being at the end of our funds, we decided to spend the night in the airport.

We found a spot under the main escalators that had room for the three of us and our backpacks. Tim, Kevin, and I settled in and pulled out our books and playing cards. We had about twelve hours overnight before our flight left. Luckily, the vending machines were in the same area, so we would not have to give up our prime spot to get dinner and breakfast.

As time passed, six other guys—aged sixteen to eighteen—joined us while we waited. Their flight was also leaving early in the morning. We introduced ourselves and were really interested to find out they were Israeli Freedom Fighters on their way to Israel.

Tim and I had an Israeli friend at our school when we were younger, but the kid had to leave school at sixteen to join the Israeli army at home and fight in the conflict. We never heard from him again after he left Geneva. I pray he survived and has been able to live a full life.

As the night progressed, we played cards, shared snacks, and told stories of our lives. I admired their bravery and conviction to drop their lives and fight for their country at such a young age; some were still in high school.

I think of them often and wonder if they survived to live out their adult lives.

It was a night I will never forget and was the perfect ending to an amazing summer vacation I shared with my brothers.

Candy for The Kids

by Barbara Emanuelson

Years ago, when my husband was a newly ordained priest, money was tight. In fact, it was that and more.

We were in the middle of upheaval, as well, because we were dealing with my devastating diagnosis of a disfiguring illness and surgery, followed by a dozen reconstructive surgeries. Insurance only covered eighty percent of the cost, leaving us more than twenty thousand dollars to pay out of pocket.

Simply put, we didn't have it. Eventually, my husband had to take a second job to pay my medical bills. Still, we counted our blessings that December as I was alive and had cheated death.

We had a two-week window of diagnosis and surgery to remove an eye tumor which would've given me brain cancer within months. We had two beautiful daughters and a roof over our heads. There was almost always something good to eat.

I was a pretty accomplished cook and knew how to pinch pennies. However, there's only so much to go around after rent, medical bills, and the day-to-day costs associated with having children. I prayed St. Nick would find a way to get to our tiny, rented house in Charlotte, North Carolina. Our parents would be generous, but I so wanted tricycles for the girls, and I didn't know if we'd be able to swing it.

A few weeks before Christmas, I had to buy food. As it happened, I had only thirty-five dollars and payday wasn't for days. Back then, it didn't cost as much to feed a family of four as it does today. Still, it wasn't a lot of money and I had to make it count.

Shopping carefully was something I could do. I bought the sale items, generics, and had flour, sugar, and eggs to bake "goodies." We actually never went without food on our table, even in those lean days.

One particular day, it was a Wednesday and I waited to see what was on sale at our local Food Lion grocery store. Chicken legs fifty-nine cents a pound for a bag. Check. Whole chickens, two dollars each. Check. Hamburger, eighty-nine a pound, check. Add the bread, a bit of lunchmeat, milk, a dozen eggs, and a pound of coffee, and I should be able to make it. Luckily, I had plenty of staple items in the pantry and freezer I could bake a batch of cookies and some banana bread and we'd get through until pay day.

I bundled up the girls that chilly morning and we headed off to the store.

It wasn't easy having two kids in tow at the grocery store. Everything they saw, they wanted. I had to say "no" to the chocolate-covered raisins and again to the jarred peanuts at the end of the produce area. I carefully avoided the snacking and cookie aisles, knowing it would be hard to say "no" to any of that.

I was familiar with the layout of the store and swiftly went about my shopping with the girls trailing behind me chitter-chattering along the way. Marking items off my handwritten list, I had it all covered. I headed to the check-out lane with both of the girls and started placing my items on the conveyor belt.

I carefully surveyed the basket, putting the most important things on first. I wasn't worried about the extra time it took because there was a gentleman ahead of me. He appeared to be ancient as his movements seemed deliberate and rather slow, though as I think on it, he was probably in his sixties.

I glanced at his items and I thought he must be having a party with all those goodies, steaks, and niceties of cake and freshly baked bread.

Gosh, that bread looks good, I thought before I looked up. My eyes met his and I smiled politely.

He seemed kind, I thought, and I remember thinking it sad he was alone.

Going about my business, I continued putting everything on the checkout belt, beginning with the meat and ending with the coffee. I knew it wasn't a necessity, but I hoped I could get it.

When the gentleman paid for his food, he insisted on bagging it himself. Proceeding to do just that, he set about his business. I watched as he carefully sorted his items and placed them in the brown paper bags.

The cashier, Renee, rang up my foods on the cash register, one item at a time. She gave me running totals every now and again, as I held my breath and prayed there was enough for the precious coffee. My little girls, aged three and four, were getting a bit rowdy, as most kids do in the store. They had been pretty well-behaved, all things considered, but I breathed a sigh of relief over how close we were to the end of this shopping day. I was certain I'd shopped wisely and had hoped the tax wouldn't send me over my budget.

My items were totaled and the cashier called out, "That's thirty-six fifty-seven, ma'am."

"How much?" I asked.

She repeated herself, not unkindly.

"Oh," I said, quietly, as I scrounged at the bottom of my purse for change. I felt the flames of embarrassment cover my face and my heart pounded out an erratic beat. Suddenly, the kiddie sounds on my left seemed deafening, and I could feel the exasperation and humiliation welling up inside of me.

There was a moment of uncomfortable silence as I stared up at the cashier.

She smiled and spoke softly. "I can take the candy off, ma'am."

"Candy?" I asked in a startled voice. "What candy?"

"This," she replied, holding up a pack of M&Ms and a Milky Way bar.

"I-I-I didn't—" I insisted, as realization dawned on me. I pivoted toward the kids, stooping low to meet their eyes. "Girls. We can't have candy today. It wasn't on our list. Mama has to put it back."

I grabbed the candy and shoved it onto the temptation shelf, anywhere it fit. My heart sank as I watched the girls' happy faces deflate. I stood up and gulped at my own sinking feelings.

Then, I heard a hearty voice say, "Whoa… what's all this change, Renee?"

It was the elderly gentleman ahead of me, who had finished loading his bags into his cart. He held in his weathered hand a few dollars and some change.

"What's that, Mr. Green?" she asked.

"This," he said handing her the extra money. "Give those little ladies that candy," he insisted in his best Santa Claus voice.

"You don't have to do that," I protested. "It's fine. *We're* fine."

He held up his hand. "Well, I'm not. I don't like carrying around a lot of singles and change." His attention returned to Renee. "How much is the candy?"

"A dollar-fifty-seven, Mr. Green."

"Here you go," he said, handing her the money. "Throw in two of those candy canes, too."

I bit my lip and forced a tear back, gazing down at my daughters.

"Girls, what do you say to this nice man?"

"Thank you," they chimed together, their happy faces shining. I retrieved the candy before tilting my head toward Mr. Green. I mouthed a barely audible, "Thanks so much."

He smiled and left the store. I heard him chuckle as he pushed his basket.

I noticed the holiday music being piped in and remembered it was Christmastime. Santa Claus had certainly visited in the Food Lion store in Charlotte, North Carolina, that day. He wasn't wearing a red suit and he didn't have a fluffy white beard. There were no reindeer and there wasn't any great sack of toys. There was simply a kindly man who gave two little girls and their mama some holiday joy.

***

We don't fret over food anymore and we own a comfortable, beautiful home in Maine. We watch our money, especially in these strange times, but we never worry about putting a meal on the table. We don't consider coffee and cream as extras and we don't mind indulging in a bit of chocolate from time-to-time.

We also don't forget those lean and meager times. Moreover, we don't forget how the kindness of a stranger can make such a difference in a person's life. And when we are able, we try to do the same for others.

I hope the generous Mr. Green is in a place of eternal jolliness and plenty. I hope he has lots of M&Ms and Milky Way bars. A candy cane or two wouldn't hurt, either.

And, I hope he knows how much his kindness meant to a struggling woman and her two darling girls. Wherever you are, Mr. Green, thank you.

Getting Lost and Found on the North Shore

by Drienie Hattingh

I was in my element. I was doing one of my favorite winter activities, cross-country skiing, in one of my favorite places in the world, The North Shore of Lake Superior, which is in the northeast corner of Minnesota. My beloved husband's birthday present to me was five glorious days on my own, doing what I loved.

I was staying at Cascade Lodge overlooking Lake Superior. "Good morning," I said to the manager in the lobby.

His name was Tom and he returned my greeting.

"I would love to make use of your cross-country skiing offer, going from one lodge to the other. How does it work?" I asked.

"You pick up skis at Solbakken Resort. It's about six miles from here. You leave your car there, then you cross-country back to Cascade where I will arrange for the forest ranger to drive you back to Solbakken where you retrieve your car."

"Great," I said, "Thank you."

"You should try and get to Solbakken before ten a.m., so you have plenty of time to ski back to Cascade before four p.m., when the sun will be setting," he said, as he rummaged through a drawer, and retrieved some forms. "You do not want to be out there in the dark. There will be a full moon tonight, but it will only rise at around seven p.m. Six hours should give you plenty of time to ski the trail, which is great. I groomed it yesterday after the fresh snow." He said with a smile. "But, if you don't make it back before dark, do not worry... we will come looking for you."

I signed a document and got into my car. As I drove past the entrance, the manager stood waving at me. I rolled down my window, and slowed down, and jokingly said, "Remember to come looking for me!"

"We will," he said. "Enjoy this beautiful day but keep the lake to your right and do not eat yellow snow."

I laughed and drove down to highway 61 and turned left to Grand Marais. As usual I went to Blue Water Café for breakfast

The previous day, I had made friends with a group of retired gentlemen who insisted I join them for breakfast every morning…. a sort of a club.

On this lovely morning, as we ate, one man asked, "What are you up to on this beautiful blue-bird day?"

"I'm going cross-country skiing, from Solbakken to Cascade Lodge."

"Great day for it," one of the old guys said. "…all that fresh snow."

"You should get a move on," someone else said, "it gets dark early this time of year."

I finished my breakfast and put my coat on with the help of one of my new friends. He put his hand on my shoulder, "Be careful out there."

"I will," I said with a smile.

I headed for the till, "See you all tomorrow."

"You get going," one of the men said, "we will get your bill.

"Gosh, you guys, thank you," I said, waving.

A chorus of goodbyes and good wishes followed me and someone called out, "Don't eat the yellow snow." They all laughed.

Well, everyone around here seems to know that one.

I drove to a mercantile shop and bought necessities for my adventure. One needs to always be prepared going out in Minnesota winters. I bought two bottles of water, some trail mix, a bar of chocolate, a packet of crackers, and, just in case, some warming pads to put in my pockets. Back in the car, I stuffed my purchases into a small backpack along with a small flask of coffee I got before I left the lodge.

I drove straight to Solbakken Resort and parked my car. I didn't want to be in the way of paying guests, so I parked in a corner of the property rather than in one of the marked guest spots. The owner, Ben, was in the lobby and gave me another form to fill out and then handed me my cross-country skis, poles, and boots. He walked with me to show me where I needed to cross highway 61 and up a hill to the cross-country trail.

"It will take you about fifteen minutes to walk up to the trail."

My watch read ten thirty a.m.

"Be safe and careful," he said.

I slung the skis and poles across my right shoulder, hooked my backpack over my left one, and grabbed the boots. I crossed the quiet highway and started up a footpath to the trail. When I got to the clearly marked trail, I put everything down and took my walking boots off, shoved them into my backpack, and put on my cross-country boots. Then, I put the skis down flat and frowned. These were not cross-country skis; these were regular downhill ones.

Oh, gosh! I removed the cross-country boots and put on my own boots again and retraced my way to the lodge. Ben was apologetic and said he would drive me up to the starting point of the trail, so I wouldn't have to walk up again. He glanced at his watch and said, "Are you sure you should still go?"

I said, "Yes, I'll be okay." It was only eleven a.m.

Ben waited at the trailhead while I put on my boots and skis and then said, "I will check at Cascade Lodge at around four to see if you made it. If not, I'll come find you. It will be quite dark before the moon comes up."

I thanked him and started skiing. It was totally amazing, surpassing all my expectations. The perfectly groomed trail stretched out ahead of me, lined with beautiful snow-covered pine trees. A Christmas card photo. The sky was a beautiful clear cold blue you only see on winter days in Minnesota. To my right, the lake was too stunning for words. The emerald blue waters were enhanced by the pure white snow in the foreground.

I glided along in a rhythmic pace enjoying every minute, marveling at my breath-taking surroundings. I breathed in deeply, enjoying the fresh cold pure air, with a hint of pine, filling my lungs. It was cold, but I was prepared, wearing several layers under my down coat, two pairs of socks, and nice warm gloves with spare ones in my backpack. The weather people said it would not go much below freezing, which was great. I stopped quite a few times, taking photos with my camera. It took a bit of time to take a photo, removing my gloves before taking a photo and then putting them back on again, but I could not resist capturing the beauty around me.

As I skied, I noticed several signs left by wildlife. I noted hoof prints from deer and moose, but there were dog-like paw prints, only much bigger. I thought it might be black bears, but surely, they would be hibernating by now. I wondered if it could be those of Timberwolves. I marveled thinking about sharing a trail with all these creatures. After another hour, I stopped and rested against a tree while I had some water and trail mix.

Back on the trail, I saw the trail now sloped down into a valley. It was fun tucking the cross-country poles under my arms and skiing swiftly down the hill. At the bottom, I came to a standstill at a creek. It was not completely frozen and was mostly covered in snow. There were rocks that would be easy to step on and cross the stream, so I removed my skies and hopped from one rock to the other until I got to the other side. However, I couldn't get my skies on again.

Suddenly, the front of the ski boots which pushed into the skis had frozen solid with ice. The temperature had dropped significantly, and I realized the sun was going down. I looked at my watch and was surprised to see it was three-thirty.

No matter how I tried. I could not get my skis on. Eventually. I threw the skis and poles back over my shoulder and decided to walk the rest of the trail. It was easier said than done. My feet and my legs disappeared into the snow right up to my knees.

I tried to keep on going for the next half an hour or so. I'd step into the snow and then lift my feet out to take another step. It was exhausting and now it was getting dark fast. I couldn't manage another step. By now, it was almost pitch dark and I couldn't even see the edges of the trail. I decided to rest for a while, even sleep for a while. I was not scared, there was nothing to worry about. I was totally alone and no one to be afraid of.

In any case, Tom and Ben would soon come for me.

It was six now and the moon would be rising in an hour. I could try again then.

I chose a tree next to the trail and settled into the snow. I poured myself a cup of coffee from the flask and ate some of the crackers and chocolate. I tore the handwarmers open to activate them and put them in my coat pockets, slipping my hands into the warmth. Soon, I drifted off to sleep.

I do not know what caused me to wake up, but I did… feeling I was being watched. My eyes opened to a fairytale scene. The full moon rose above the snow-covered pine trees and everything was bathed in its bright light. The trees were clearly visible and so was the trail. Several deer crossed in front of me. I marveled in being totally alone, the only one, right there, at *that* stunning moment, watching this scene unfolding in front of me. *I was part of it all.*

I thanked God for this moment and for my wonderful husband.

I got up, shook the snow off, and gathered my things. I continued the laborious journey through the deep snow. I had renewed energy. Half an hour later, I felt the hard surface of a paved road under my boots.

Thank God!

I turned toward the lake knowing the road would take me down to Highway 61. Once there, I could walk the rest of the way to Cascade Lodge. The road was silent and devoid of any cars. I had been trekking for about fifteen minutes when I heard a car. Soon, a small vehicle stopped next to me and the driver rolled the window down.

An elderly lady peeked out the window. She smiled broadly and said, "What are you doing here, in the middle of nowhere, with skis over your shoulder?"

I was about to answer her when she said, "Wait! Heavens to Betsy, are you the woman from Africa who's lost, and everyone is praying for?"

I looked at her in astonishment. "Well… I'm not really lost, but yes, it could be me, I guess."

"Get in, sweetie," she said. "Throw your stuff on the back seat and let's go. There are people out searching

for you and we have to put all those praying Lutherans'
minds to rest."

Grateful, I climbed into her warm car.

"So, tell me," she said. "What happened?"

When I finished relaying my escapades, she shook
her head and laughed.

"Well, everyone up and down the shore knows
about you and is praying for you. The phone lines were
buzzing, let me tell you. When it got dark, Tom called
and asked Ben if he could see if your car was still in the
parking lot. He said he couldn't, then, when you didn't
show up at Cascade, Ben checked again and then found
your car." She glanced and me and said pointedly, "It
was not parked in the parking area."

She continued, "They thought you were lost, in
trouble, or had fallen and broken an ankle. They loaded
up their snowmobiles with leg splints and supplies. Tom
started from Cascade and Ben from Solbakken, thinking
they would cover the whole trail. They ended up in the
middle, where you apparently took a nap."

I listened to her in awe, feeling extremely foolish.
"Really? Oh, my goodness. I am so sorry… I do not know
what to say…"

She giggled a bit, "Do you know, people were not only praying for you, God even sent someone to watch over you while you were sleeping?"

What is she talking about?

I started shivering as the ice and snow on my jeans, coat, and gloves were starting to melt. With clattering teeth, I asked, "What?" My mind flashed to the feeling of being watched.

"Yes, my dear," she said. "Tom and Ben are good trackers. They saw your imprint in the snow where you slept and even guessed by the deepness of the dent in the snow, that you rested there for about an hour. What they also saw was paw marks of five timber wolves, right at the same tree where you were sleeping. They said the wolves must have been there for at least half an hour."

"Timberwolves?"

"Yes, but do not worry, they would not have harmed you. Like I said, they watched over you."

As we came into the lobby of Cascade Lodge, it was filled with locals who turned around and cheered. Some even hugged me.

My rescue angel gave me a hug and left. I never even got her name.

A man immediately got on a walkie talkie and I heard him say, "She's here! She's cold, but she's fine, no broken legs."

Another man called the police and yet another called a pastor, saying "Please let everyone know we can change our prayers to praise now."

I stood there shivering, listening to all these wonderful, wonderful people who did so much for me... a complete stranger.

A woman helped me to remove my wet coat and boots and draped a blanket over my shoulders. She made me sit in a chair. Someone else pushed a mug of hot coffee into my shaking hands and placed a bowl of soup and warm biscuits on a table next to me.

Tom and Ben entered the lobby and both hugged me. I kept on thanking them over and over.

"Well," Tom said, "all's well that ends well, right?" He smiled, "And what about them wolves?! Who would have guessed you were off to such an adventure this morning?" He asked for my keys and he and Ben drove to Solbakken to get my car.

After some sips of the coffee and munching on a biscuit, I related my whole story to a captive audience.

It was with a thankful heart I closed the door after Tom left that night. I turned around and went up the stairs to my bedroom. I said my prayers standing at the window, gazing over the big seemingly never-ending lake with a full moon above it. After asking God to keep His hand of protection over my beloved husband and children, I thanked God for strangers who cared for strangers… and for sending watchdogs, too.

A Pocket Full of Coins

by Lynda West Scott

A woman muttering to herself walked toward me along a fashionable street as I headed to my hair appointment. Her eyes didn't leave the sidewalk in front of her and I wondered if she even knew she passed me. She seemed out of place in this neighborhood with her drab clothing, but she didn't look disheveled or homeless.

Thirty seconds or so later, footsteps echoed along the sidewalk behind me, coming quickly in my direction. This startled me as no one besides the woman and I had been on this side of the street. I turned to see who it might be and the woman nearly bumped into me.

Perhaps I had been wrong about her being homeless. Upon a *much* closer look, her tangle of gray hair and travel-worn clothing was evident. She didn't move to step around me, rather she stood fixed with her eyes averted.

"I need two dollars for the bus," she said in a squeaky voice.

I wondered if it was a statement, question, or a request. Definitely the latter.

It had been a very long time since I rode a city bus, although I did use our city's light rail system. In truth, I had no idea what a bus ticket might cost.

Years ago, as a six-year-old kid, I had become well-versed in public transportation and transferring from bus-to-bus while traveling to and from a private school. Every school-day morning, my mother sent me on my way with two nickels: one for the trip to school and one for the ride home.

My greatest fear became reality one day when she told me she only had ten pennies and I would need to be careful not to lose any. All went well on the ride to school; however, by the time several friends and I got to the bus stop that afternoon, only four pennies remained in my lunch pail. I wailed in panic.

My friends calmed me down and we devised a plan. I entered the bus first and put one penny in the collection box. I watched the rolling surface sweep it into the hidden compartment below. I fidgeted with my remaining pennies and "allowed" my classmates to drop their fare in the box between each of my coins. After depositing my last penny, and assured we had outsmarted the bus driver, I started down the aisle to join my friends.

A hand tugging on my skirt kept me from progressing away from the driver, who barked: "Not so fast. Where's your fifth penny?"

Tears immediately scrolled down my cheeks and the hand on my skirt relaxed when I promised I would bring the missing penny the next day. He was not happy. "Don't forget it or I won't let you on the bus again."

I probably cried all the way home. And, I certainly had eleven cents with me the next day. The importance of a penny never left me after that bus ride.

Remembering this experience kindled compassion for this woman, though I still couldn't believe bus fare had increased to two dollars. Or, perhaps it cost more, and the woman only needed two dollars to make up the difference.

A dilemma raced through my thoughts. I had two dollars in my wallet a few days ago, but I had spent them, hadn't I? I knew for certain I had a twenty. Two dollars was one thing, but I wasn't about to give her a twenty. If I waited for the bus with her, I'd miss my appointment.

What to do? I couldn't ignore her plight. I had been accumulating a lot of change. I intended to add it to my parking meter fund in the cubby of my car console, but I hadn't done it yet, so...

I removed my coin purse and said, "I don't have any bills, but there must be over two dollars in coins here." I sorted through them picking out a few buttons, a paperclip, and a Lego. I tipped the rest into her outstretched hands, filling them to near overflowing. Good deed done; I closed the purse.

"Have a good day."

Her eyes remained fixed on her hands loaded with coins, which, much to my chagrin, seemed to contain a lot of pennies. Before I took a step, she said, "Thank you, Lynda."

The shock at hearing my name from a woman I had never met propelled me away from her and into the shop without a backward glance.

Once seated in the waiting area, I considered her words. I knew I hadn't misheard her. I had not opened my wallet, so there was no chance she saw my ID. How did she know my name?

Guilt set in. Had I been so eager to dismiss her that I assumed I had two dollars in change in my purse? I could have entered the salon and asked for change for my twenty to be sure she had enough. Anxiety left me poor company for my stylist, whose words belied belief in my story…

"She must have seen your ID…"

"Maybe you introduced yourself…"

When I left the salon, I fairly fled to my lunch appointment with my mother-in-law, Maralyn. This wise woman had guided me through many life events. She would understand and help lift me out of this funk.

However, if I thought she would coddle me and tell me I had done my best, I was wrong. After listening to my story, she said, "Honey, she knew your name. You were being tested."

Her statement only heightened my distress. Maralyn's beliefs might have differed from mine, yet I accepted things sometimes occurred with no reasonable explanation. Thoughts tumbled through my mind.

What if it was a test? What if the coins I had given her amounted to less than two dollars? What if I only thought I had spent those two dollars?

I grabbed my wallet from my purse and opened the snap to where I stored my cash. Next to the twenty-dollar bill were two dollars. Exactly what the woman had asked for.

I gasped, holding up the one-dollar bills for Maralyn to see.

"I failed the test."

The Missing Wedding Ring

by Mary Pettersen

I traveled from Williston, North Dakota to St. Paul, Minnesota on the Amtrak Empire Builder. It was a trip my husband and I had made many times since moving to Williston in 2011, but on this trip, I was by myself. I even had the sleeper car roomette all to myself and meals in the dining car.

At breakfast, I moved to leave the table and happened to glance down at my hand.

My wedding ring was gone.

This was my original wedding ring I always wore on a necklace along with other treasured charms. My necklace had been repaired, so I decided to wear the small band on my pinky finger where it now fit. The monetary value of the ring was minimal, but the sentimental value was priceless.

Now it was… *gone?*

The attendant immediately helped in the search through the bedding. She hunted on the floor which was no easy task in the tiny roomette.

No ring.

She searched the halls and the floor beneath the table where I sat for breakfast.

No ring.

Now, I sat in the roomette staring out the window trying to enjoy the scenery for the final two hours of my journey. I resigned myself to the fact that my precious ring was gone.

Before my final stop, my attendant popped her head into my room.

She held out her hand.

I could not believe my eyes. In the palm of her hand lay my tiny gold band.

"Where did you find it?"

"On the floor of the shower," she told me with delight.

It apparently had slipped off my soapy hand.

With trembling fingers, I picked up the ring from her hand and held it close to my heart. My eyes filled with tears and I gave her a huge hug.

The woman didn't have to keep searching for my ring, but she knew how much it meant to me.

What an angel.

I instantly put the ring back on my necklace and haven't taken it off since.

Tom

by Eugene Hattingh

In the summer of 1995, my friends, Ted and Rachel, and I came up with a crazy idea: Hitchhike around the USA.

We would start in Minnesota, go west to Washington, down to California, crossing the southwest, across the south to Florida, up to Maine and then back to Minnesota. Obviously, it would take several months, and the plan was to work along the way for money to keep the adventure going.

Well, we made it to California and stayed there for a while in Pismo Beach. One-by-one, we all returned to Minnesota.

While the trip all the way around the country was a failure, it was the most exciting thing I've ever done, and there were several thrilling things that happened along the way.

We met so many interesting people and saw so much. There was a woman who let us camp in her backyard. Another woman allowed us to ride in her semi-truck with her and her dog. There was the cop who wrote citations for us hitchhiking on a highway. We witnessed to two different fires at separate places we stayed. We lived through the miserable rains of Washington and Oregon. We met some cute girls along the way. We snuck into campsites late at night and left before the sun came up, so we didn't have to pay. We got abducted by aliens. We learned new sayings like, "it's raining like a cow pissing on a flat rock." We visited Wall Drug, Mount Rushmore, and the Crazy Horse Memorial. We went up the Space Needle for an extremely expensive lunch and touched the Pacific Ocean for the first time.

Okay, all of it is true except one thing.

However, my favorite memory of the whole journey was meeting a man named Tom.

Spending twenty-four hours a day with two other people can become a problem. While in Oregon, the three of us argued quite a bit. We decided we needed to split up for a while and continue the adventure by ourselves.

The plan was to meet up again in San Francisco.

Ted and Rachel headed off and I stayed back for a bit. When I eventually went out to the highway, I thought it would be a while before I got a ride. However, within a minute of raising my thumb, a man in a truck stopped.

His name was Tom and lived somewhere in Oregon. He was on his way to San Francisco. He told me when he was younger, he used to hitchhike up and down the west coast all the time. So that's why he decided to pick me up.

We drove for a while and then stopped for dinner. Tom paid for both of us. Now, this was back in the day before there was such a thing as a cell phone. So, me, Ted and Rachel said we would keep in touch by calling my parents collect.

While at the restaurant with Tom, I called my parents. Mom answered.

She was obviously happy to hear from her son. "Eugene, how are you? Where are you? Are you okay?"

I assured her I am fine and told her where I was.

"Rachel called," Mom said. "She sounded sad and troubled. She did not say much, but apparently she had a bad experience."

I was not happy to hear this. I had been extremely concerned that she was on her own.

"Where is she?" I asked. "Did she say?"

"Yes, she was dropped off at a youth hostel."

My mom told me where the youth hostel was, and it turned out that it was about twenty miles south of the restaurant Tom and I were at. What are the chances.

I asked Tom if we could go pick Rachel up. He said yes and we headed off to the hostel.

I will always remember Rachel's face when I entered the youth hostel. She was on a pay phone and seemed frustrated. She hung up and spun around. As soon as she saw me, she smiled and burst out crying.

We hugged and I told her we had a ride to San Francisco. She was so relieved. We hopped into Tom's truck and headed south.

Tom's plan was to drive through the night, but he asked if we had ever seen the Redwoods. Neither of us had.

"You need to see them," he said. With that, we decided to get a motel, get some rest and visit the Redwoods first thing. Tom even paid for the room.

The next morning, we went to the Redwoods. It was a beautiful sight I will always remember. We even drove through the one hollowed-out redwood. I still have the picture of Rachel, Tom, and me standing in front of his truck parked inside the tree. It truly was unbelievable.

I stood there, looking up at those monstrous redwoods thinking it was so majestic and I was so... small.

As we neared San Francisco, we stopped at a lookout sight before crossing the Golden Gate Bridge. It was an amazing view as we looked down on the bridge and the rolling hills in San Francisco. It was simply spectacular.

Tom drove us into China Town and sprung for Chinese restaurant. When we came in, many of the workers yelled out his name. It was surprising and funny.

We sat down at a big round table where Tom ordered a bunch of food that covered the whole table. Tom paid again and handed the bag of leftovers to us.

I called my parents from the restaurant to see if anyone had heard from Ted. He was actually right there, at a youth hostel back on the north side of the Golden Gate Bridge. Tom drove us to the hostel and dropped us off, then waved goodbye.

It's funny thinking back now. Ted, Rachel, and I had split up the day before, and now we were all so excited to be back together again.

We met many interesting people on our grand adventure, but for me Tom tops the list. I mean, it's twenty-five years later and I still remember his name. He went out of his way to make our trip even more special. For a stranger to spend so much time and money on us truly showed me the kindness of people in the USA, the greatest country in the world.

Paris Metro Flash Mob

by Marley Gibson

Ahhh… Paris. Romantic walks through the Tulleries, strolling hand-in-hand around the Louvre, dinner at the café with bread, wine, and escargot, and topping the evening off with a kiss at the top of the Eiffel Tower.

In December 2018, I planned an end-of-the-year getaway for my husband, Patrick, and me and couldn't think of any better place than Paris. It had been a trying and emotional year with the loss of my brother and moving my elderly mother to Savannah. With all the struggles, this was the perfect prescription we needed.

However, by the time mid-December rolled around, Paris was almost two months into their Yellow Vests Movement, a populist, grassroots protest against the

French president demanding economic justice. These protests started out peacefully, but sadly became violent with people busting out store windows, breaking ATMs, and spray-painting graffiti. Some Paris Metro stations were closed on the weekend, as were select museums and tours. Despite this, we made the best of it.

Thus far, our trip had been free of the protests and police presence—Paris is huge, so it's possible to avoid certain areas. Our guide recommended we see Sainte Chappelle—a thirteenth century gothic chapel with some of Paris' most exquisite stained glass. Unfortunately, for safety sake, they were closed, and we were sorely disappointed. This happened with several things that particular day and we were... annoyed.

Feeling a bit defeated, we decided to return to our apartment to regroup, refresh, and figure out what was actually open. It was freezing cold and our gloves and scarves weren't cutting it.

"I'm so cold, my eyelashes hurt," I moaned.

Patrick commiserated. "I'm miserable."

Bitterly, we stepped into the station for the Paris Metro Line 9 in the direction of our stop, Alma-Marceau, a ten-minute walk from our accommodations.

When the doors *swooooshed* open, we were immediately met with loud Christmas music piping out from the car. People were dressed in festive sweaters, wearing gold and silver tinsel, headbands with ornaments, and handing out drinks and snacks for anyone moving onto the train. Caroling rang out. Laughter echoed everywhere. They smiled and waved us in to join the festivities.

What was going on?

They chattered fast and furiously in exquisite French, as if I understood everything. All I could do was grin like a complete idiot. A happy one.

Immediately, our spirits lifted. We no longer cared about the missed exhibits or the frigid weather, or even how we were feeling sorry for ourselves. *Get over it.* We were in Paris! The City of Lights. The City of Love. So much love and friendship and spirit abounded.

"This is the coolest thing ever," Patrick shouted while recording the whole event.

These lovely folks didn't speak much English and my French… well, I know a lot of cooking terms and small phrases, so we did the best we could using hand motions, broken language, and smiling.

We gleaned they were co-workers who decided to make their holiday office party a metro-riding flash mob to spread seasonal cheer on a Friday night. We joined in instantaneously, singing and dancing and sharing in the wonderful atmosphere.

People came and went, got on and off, and we bellowed along with everyone else, "Merry Christmas" and "Joyeux Noël." There was clapping and cheering and so many smiles. Love and holiday spirit overflowed.

We weren't French or American.

We weren't foreigners or countryman.

We weren't even strangers.

We were people.

Human. One beautiful, spontaneous, celebratory display of the joy of the season and what happens when folks come together with elation in their hearts to share a moment.

We only needed to ride about five stops, but we ended up missing our stop — twice — and riding to the end of the line with this amazing group. We helped greet newcomers as they entered the train and we handed out drinks and snacks. We danced, we sang, and we made friends on social media and swapped pictures and video of the night.

So often, we get so involved in disappointments around us and focusing on the negative instead of finding the happiness in *any* situation. There's always something positive and inspiring around us, all we have to do is peak around and participate.

When the train hissed into Alma-Marceau stop for a third time, we reluctantly slipped away, waving goodbye to our new friends and a reminiscence we'd never forget. That night, perhaps we did our part for diplomacy, humanity, and the spirit of mankind. We shared and celebrated and were joyful in the moment. It lasted about an hour, but it made an indelible mark on our hearts.

Every now and then, when everything goes awry and not like you planned, you *juuuuuust* might end up having the best time of your life.

Silver Linings during COVID-19

Carolyn Campbell...

During the pandemic, I learned that you don't have to be productive during quarantine. Sometimes it's enough to just focus on taking care of yourself and those you love. One of my favorite quotes is, "Be gentle with yourself, because life isn't always gentle with you."

Terry Clancy...

The happiest and most exciting thing to happen to me during the pandemic is the birth of my first grandchild on September 9, 2020. Her name is Azralia Xavine Tabaracci. I totally captivated by this small human. I can simply sit and watch her all day. I thought I would never experience being a *grandparent. She is a perfect blend of both her parents, my Son and Daughter in Law. I can't wait to start my Nonna duties. I am only allowed 1 visit per week for no more than 2 hours per COVID restrictions. I am looking forward to the time I can teach her to cook and bake.*

Barbara Emanuelson…

During the COVID-19 crisis, I learned to put myself and my well-being at the forefront. With the love and support of my husband, I embarked on lifestyle changes that included a healthy and balanced diet, exercise, deeper spirituality, and a quieter, more settled mind. I'm learning to live a life that's conducive to this goal. Some days are harder than others. But I'm learning that I'm worth it. I rely more on God, and less on myself. Living in His service includes taking care of myself. After all, He wants me to be the best version of me.

Doug Gibson…

This year COVID-19 cost our family a much-anticipated trip to Hungary. However, I arranged a reunion of several close friends from high school in Long Beach, Calif. It was a wonderful experience reconnecting with these people, some for the first time in thirty-eight years.

Marley Gibson…

As with many families, 2020 has not been kind to our household. Our tour business had to close for six months, and despite our extreme carefulness outside the house, we both contracted COVID-19. However, we made the best of it — together — reading, writing, watching documentaries, painting, playing with lasers, entertaining the kitties. We made it through thanks to our crazy love for each other. Not that I didn't know that before COVID.

Mette Harrison...

We had a homeless teen staying with us during the pandemic, a friend of my youngest son who was a senior, and so we played games nearly every night. It was the only way I guess my son would have bothered to play with us, since his options were gone. My favorite memory of the pandemic by far.

Drienie Hattingh...

The whole world is in this together. In a weird way, this knowledge was and is comforting. My husband, Johan, who has heart failure, and I, have been isolating since March 7th and will be until a vaccine is found. After being deeply involved with our children and grandsons, we can now only visit 'through the window.' In many ways, isolation has been a blessing. Just seeing my children and grandsons beloved faces, outside our glass sliding doors, makes me love them even more. Johan and I've appreciated each other much more. Every meal is now a special occasion. I have made amazing new recipes and we dine outside on our porch or have picnics on the beach. We also have movie nights. I am blessed having children who love us enough to keep their distance, but I do miss my grandsons' hugs... so much.

Eugene Hattingh…

Before the pandemic started, I really didn't go out much because I've been working from home for many years, so I am lucky in that regard. I guess I miss playing racquetball, but that is a sport that might eventually die out because no one would want to be in a closed court with anyone else. I used to get fast food all the time, but now my fiancé cooks for us every day, so that's a good thing. Plus, the food is actually much better than burgers and fries, in both taste and nutritional value.

Karen Jelinek…

Spending so much time with family has been more of a blessing than a burden. We've found some new games to learn and play together (board, dice, card, etc.). This time has also allowed us all to slow down and enjoy each other and what we have.

Celeste Kuun…

Lockdown sucked! It was hard to be away from my learners, who depend on school for meals and an escape from nightmarish circumstances at home. Through lockdown, I learned to appreciate what I have. I am thankful for a steady income, a loving family, technology to keep in contact with loved ones and hobbies, like writing and drawing, to keep me sane. (I am very much an indoorsy person). I also learned that life is full of beauty- if only we take the time to see it.

Alex Montanez…

After the pandemic began, I felt the need to put out a positive message to all my friends and family. At that point, my daily podcast was born, and I received so many compliments from people telling me how much it meant to them, to be able to see someone that they know, providing positive vibes and encouragement. I continue to do my daily podcasts today.

Christy Monson…

The pandemic has been a blessing in my life. I've had the opportunity to have all my children in my home. We've had wonderful discussions and great times together. We hold Zoom meetings twice a month, so we are together more now than before the pandemic.

Penny Ogle…

Grandchildren often say, "I love you Grandma" and seal it with a hug. But, this past year, my grandchildren showed me their love by doing what they could to keep me safe. They missed out on college graduation ceremonies, they presented plays via zoom rather than to an audience, and they stood on the porch singing Happy Birthday rather than expose me to a potential virus. Our children brought groceries and wiped them down before bringing them into our house. The most important thing was, no matter what they missed out on…. they never stopped saying I love you.

Mary Pettersen…

When the people of the United States were beginning to "Stay at Home" we had just returned from three months in Mexico. It was so good to be home on the prairie where we knew if we needed care, we would be able to receive it. Winter was still upon us, so we hunkered down in our little schoolhouse home on the prairie. We self-quarantined for the required fourteen days and truly enjoyed taking walks on our section line road where there was no chance of meeting anyone. Our dog loved it, too. Our chickens provided eggs daily and we were glad for Mark's hunting last fall. It was truly a treasured time together.

Lynda West Scott…

COVID-19 seemed to drape a dark veil over my life, and then California experienced a mega four-hour, dramatically beautiful, but deadly lightening display that lit hundreds of fires. After twenty-one days of evacuation, returning to a home that still stood, even if it was in the midst of skeleton-blackened trees, put my petty COVID-19 feelings of isolation into perspective. Nearly a thousand families in my area were left without their homes. Six of us seventy-plus year-old neighbors had been welcomed in by a couple with a large home when our mandatory evacuation order arrived. In the twenty-one days we remained together, we learned to laugh at Lonny, who has Alzheimer and would wander a lot, and a world-traveler who wouldn't eat the crusts on her sandwiches, or the foibles of singing husbands. We dined like royalty and perhaps drank too much wine, but as dark as days could be without knowing if we had homes to return to, when the evacuation order was lifted, all eight of us realized how much we had come to care for each other and how blessed we were to share this time together.

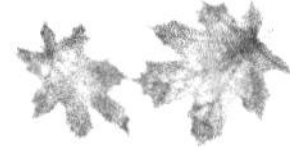

Anne Sinno…

The 2020 Pandemic has given a new outlook to cooking for my husband and myself. We learned to enjoy cooking together at home instead of eating out. Having eaten out most of the time, after a few months, we now choose to cook together rather than eat out. We are both pleasantly surprised.

Wendy Toliver....

One of the silver linings of the pandemic is, it helped my youngest son discover his love of fly-fishing. It's given him goals — from learning the skills from his grandfather and watching videos, to earning money to buy the equipment. He's become quite the accomplished angler!

Sherry Wallwork...

This pandemic has taught me that quiet is lovely, and slow is joyful. Because in the slow and the quiet, you notice little things that are incredibly lovely. Things that were there all the time, but you were rushing around and past them to get somewhere. I have re-discovered reading, and reflecting, and old pictures, and slow cooking, and myself, in this place that is my home. I'll be honest, I don't hate it.

Dimitria Van Leeuwen…

My roommate and I learned 'cups' and became proficient enough to perform it even after a few glasses of wine! And I learned that dogs and cats are really good company. I also learned that online community can be real community. And that humans can be brilliant and creative when faced with a challenge.

Margaret Zeemer…

Who could imagine that such a calamity would occur in our lifetime? COVID-19 has struck at the core of every facet of our society and it has been a challenge to rise to the occasion and do what it takes until a safe vaccine is secured. In the meantime, I stay at home as much as I can and always wear a mask when I go out, wash hands and read, read, read. My local library is my best friend.

Drienie Hattingh was born and raised in South Africa. She is an award-winning author, columnist, journalist, and is the author of two books and compiled and published five anthologies: *Forever Friends. A Glass Slipper for Christmas. The Best Worst Christmas Ever, Tales from Two-Bit Street and Beyond, Part I. Tales from Two-Bit Street and Beyond, Part II, Tales from The Wasatch and Beyond. Tales from Ogden Canyon and Beyond.* Except for writing, one of Drienie's passions is to help fellow authors publish their books. Drienie has three children and two grandsons. In her spare time, she loves to visit and care for her two grandsons and knit for family and friends. Drienie lives in Gig Harbor, Washington with her husband, Johan. They will be celebrating their 50th anniversary in November 2020.

Carolyn Campbell is the author of three nationally published books and more than 900 magazine articles. She is also a frequently requested speaker about writing topics and has also presented a humorous talk about home organization to over 200 women's and humanitarian organizations.

Terry Clancy grew up all over. Her dad worked for Caterpillar Tractor and were transferred every two years as Terry was growing up. She spent six-and-a-half years in Geneva, Switzerland. Books were her best friends. She was never alone as long as she had a book with her. Terry worked at a local bookstore in Ogden, Utah for ten years, where she lives. She has two children and a granddaughter.

Barbara Emanuelson is retired educator and published author of adult historical fiction, YA historical fiction/fantasy, paranormal, and personal narrative. In addition to writing, she enjoys gardening, cooking, baking, playing her musical instruments, and singing.

She is the mother of three adult daughters and wife of an Orthodox Christian priest. Barbara currently makes her home in Auburn, Maine.

Doug Gibson is a retired journalist who lives in Ogden, Utah. He now reviews business taxes for the Internal Revenue Service. He and his wife Kati have three children. Doug also maintains four active blogs.

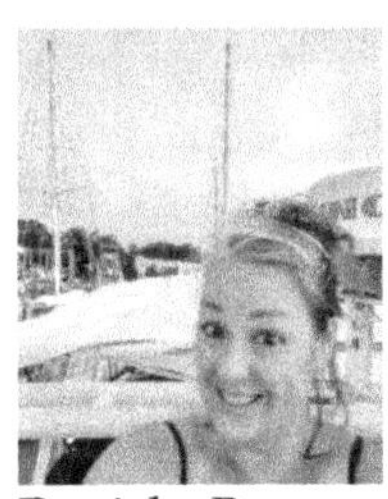

Marley Gibson is a multi-published author of young adult, women's fiction, and many non-fiction books. She is also a freelance editor and author mentor. She and her husband, Patrick Burns, live in Savannah, Georgia, with their rescue kitties, Madison and Boo, and run a tour company, Exploration Point, and a tour boat, *Aqua Therapy*.

Mette Ivie Harrison is the author of the Linda Wallheim mystery series set in Mormon, Utah. She's also written many YA fantasies, including The Princess and the Hound. She is an autist.

Eugene Hattingh was voted sexiest man alive four years in a row until Brad Pitt came along. He received a bachelor's degree in advertising from the Academy of Art in San Francisco and is currently working in online retail. He lives with his fiancée, Shu, and their cat, Tabby, north of Seattle. He has written several screenplays that received high accolades from those who've read them. He is the only one who has read them. His all-time favorite show is *Friends*, movie, *The Godfather*, and band, Def Leppard.

Karen Jelinek is a thirty-six-year-old substitute teacher. She loves reading, playing ice hockey, square dancing, watching movies, and going to her family's log cabin in Wisconsin. She lives in Woodbury, Minnesota with her rescue cat, Jupiter Rambo.

Celeste Kuun is a language teacher in Johannesburg, South Africa. Travelling is her passion but a hobby she scarcely can afford (let's blame a poor exchange rate!). So instead she fills her spare time with tea, cats, music and books.

This is the first time Celeste have written short stories for an anthology. She hopes to soon be invited to accept her Nobel Prize for Literature. As you can tell, she has a good sense of humor.

Christy Monson lives in Ogden, Utah. She is a retired family therapist and has published several books: Non Fiction: *Finding Peach in Times of Tragedy, Family Talk, Love, Hugs, and Hope, Becoming Free, A Woman's Guide to Internal Strength, Stand Up to Sexting,* and *An Open Conversation Between Parents and Kids; and fiction: Banished.* She can be found online at: www.christymonson.com, twitter.com@ChristyMonson, www.christymonson.blogspot.com, www.facebook.com/christymonsonauthor

Alex Montanez loves life even when it's tough. He likes to create and challenge himself to new and exciting mediums. He tried writing, acting, singing, photography, storytelling, podcasts, comedy. He did not succeed in all of these things but is never afraid to fail and continues to experience all life has to offer.

 **Penny Ogle** believes in blooming where planted. This attitude afforded her the opportunity to live and work in many places. She earned a BSS in Business from George Mason University two weeks prior to their oldest graduating from high school. Penny retired in 2019 and now explores all of the adventures ignored while dutifully meeting the requirements of a career. She enjoys writing. This is her second non-fiction story.

 **Mary Pettersen** lives on the North Dakota prairie with her husband Mark, Golden Retriever, Ole, and their rescued cat Frozen. Their home is a renovated 100-year-old one-room schoolhouse which they moved from its original location to the middle of a wheat field. They also have a cabin on Crane Lake in Minnesota at the entrance to Voyageurs National Park where they see the sunrise through the majestic pines over the lake. They have two daughters and two grandchildren. Her stories in *Fleeting Encounters* are her first to be published.

 **Lynda West Scott** won awards for her writing in high school and first place for her novel from the Utah League of Writers. She has written magazine articles, co-published three anthologies, contributed ten stories to seven anthology books, and her debut novel, *Without Reason* is scheduled for publication in 2021.

 **Anne Sinno** grew up on the lakes of Minnesota. After moving to Phoenix, she traveled the US, partnering with financial advisors to build their businesses as a retirement planning resource. She and her husband, Barry, started Datum Charters, offering private yacht trips all over the world. This is her first published story.

 **Wendy Toliver.** It's not hard to find creative inspiration when surrounded by mountain and lake views from her Utah home.. She is a bestselling, award-winning novelist, as well as essayist, writing coach, and bad poet. She is the author of *The Secret Life of a Teenage Siren*, *Miss Match*, *Lifted*, and two *Disney novels, Red's Untold Tale*, and *Regina Rising.*

Dimitria Van Leeuwen is an artist who divides her time between the stunning deserts of Southern Utah and the culturally vivid Mexico City. She loves to write and her stories have been published in four anthologies, *Tales from Ogden Canyon and Beyond*, *Tales from Two-Bit Street and Beyond, Part I*, and *Part II*, and *Tales from The Wasatch and Beyond*. She has also designed and produced many book covers for fiction and non-fiction authors.

Sherry (Hogg) Wallwork loves writing for fun. Her picture book, *Child of Mine*, a mommy love story, covers her favorite topic...the unstoppable, indestructible, and infinite nature of a mother's love. She loved raising her four amazing children in Utah's beautiful Ogden Valley, and is currently enjoying her dream job, teaching 7th grade English. Sherry resides in Pleasant View with her husband Sid and her ridiculously adorable basset Sadie. Sherry has stories published in two spooky anthologies, *Tales from Ogden Canyon and Beyond* and *Tales from The Wasatch and Beyond*.

Margaret Zeemer is a retired owner of the Wisebird Bookery, a much loved iconic bookstore in Ogden, Utah. She moved here from England back in 1966 and is now spending her time traveling the world and writing about her travels. When at home she lives with her Pomeranian daughter, Eleanor. She has a short story published in The Best Worst Christmas Ever.